C000177377

STAFFORDSHIRE
PARISH CHURCHES

STAFFORDSHIRE PARISH CHURCHES

by John Leonard

*With a foreword by
the Rt. Revd. Keith Sutton, Bishop of Lichfield*

Breedon Books
Publishing Company
Derby

First published in Great Britain by
The Breedon Books Publishing Company Limited
44 Friar Gate, Derby, DE1 1DA.
1995

© John Leonard 1995

All Rights Reserved. No part of this publication may be reproduced, stored in a retrieval system, or transmitted in any form, or by any means, electronic, mechanical, photocopying, recording or otherwise without the prior permission in writing of the Copyright holders, nor be otherwise circulated in any form or binding or cover other than in which it is published and without a similar condition being imposed on the subsequent publisher.

By the same author:
Derbyshire Parish Churches
Shropshire Parish Churches

But let my due feet never fail
To walk the studious cloister's pale,
And love the high embowed roof,
With antique pillars massy-proof,
And storied windows richly dight,
Casting a dim religious light.
There let the pealing organ blow
To the full-voiced quire below
In service high and anthems clear,
As may with sweetness, through mine ear,
Dissolve me into ecstasies,
And bring all Heaven before mine eyes.

J. Milton   Il Penseroso

For Andrew and Isabel

All royalties from the sale of this book will be devoted to the Church Urban Fund of the Diocese of Lichfield.

ISBN 1 83983 003 X
Cover printed by Premier Print, Nottingham.
Printed and bound by Hillman Printers, Frome, Somerset.

Contents

Introduction: Visiting Staffordshire churches   7

The Anglo-Saxon Church in Staffordshire   9

The Arrival of the Normans   13
The Priory Church of St Mary, TUTBURY   14
St Chad, STAFFORD   16

The Early English Style – the Thirteenth Century 18
St Lawrence, COPPENHALL   19
Holy Trinity, ECCLESHALL   20

The Decorated Style – the Fourteenth Century   22
St Andrew, CLIFTON CAMPVILLE   24

The Perpendicular Style – 1350-1550   26
St James, BARTON-UNDER-NEEDWOOD   27

The Seventeenth Century   29
St Peter, BROUGHTON   29
St Mary, INGESTRE   30

The Eighteenth Century   32
St John, WOLVERHAMPTON   32
St Luke, SHARESHILL   33

The Nineteenth and Twentieth Centuries   34
St Matthew, WALSALL   34
All Saints, DENSTONE   36
Holy Angels, HOAR CROSS   37

The Collegiate Churches   39
St Laurence, GNOSALL   39
St Michael, PENKRIDGE   40
St Mary, STAFFORD   42
St Editha, TAMWORTH   43
St Michael and All Angels, TETTENHALL   46
St Peter, WOLVERHAMPTON   47

Works of Art in Staffordshire Churches   49
Norman fonts   49
The Swynnerton Statue   50
Monumental Effigies 1270-1700   51
Medieval stained glass   60
Medieval screens   64
Seventeenth-century pulpits   66
Altar-rails, choir-stalls, bench-ends, box-pews   69

Churches in the Regions of Staffordshire   71

The Northern Uplands   71
St Peter, ALSTONEFIELD   71
St Bartholomew, BLORE   73
St Edward, CHEDDLETON   74
St Michael, HORTON   75
Holy Cross, ILAM   75
St Edward the Confessor, LEEK   76
St John the Baptist, MAYFIELD   77
All Saints, OKEOVER   78
St Lawrence, RUSHTON SPENCER   79
St James and St Bartholomew, WATERFALL   81

The Environs of the Potteries   82
St James, AUDLEY   82
St Margaret, BETLEY   83
St Leonard, BRADLEY-IN-THE-MOORS   83
St Mary, CHECKLEY   84
St Margaret, DRAYCOTT-IN-THE-MOORS   85
All Saints, LEIGH   86
All Saints, MADELEY   87
All Saints, SANDON   88
St Michael, STONE   89
St John, STOWE-BY-CHARTLEY   90
St Mary, SWYNNERTON   91

The West   92
St John the Baptist, ASHLEY   92
St Mary, BLYMHILL   92
St Mary and All Saints, BRADLEY   93
All Saints, CHEBSEY   94
St Editha, CHURCH EATON   95
All Saints, FORTON   95
St Mary, HIGH OFFLEY   96
All Saints, LAPLEY   96
St Peter, NORBURY   97
St Chad, SEIGHFORD   98
St Andrew, WESTON-UNDER-LIZARD   98

The Forest of Needwood   100
All Saints, ALREWAS   100
St Leonard, BLITHFIELD   101
St Michael, HAMSTALL RIDWARE   102
St Werburgh, HANBURY   103
St Nicholas, MAVESYN RIDWARE   105
St Mary, ROLLESTON   106
St Michael, TATENHILL   106
St Leonard, WYCHNOR   107

The South-east   108
St John, ARMITAGE   108
St John the Baptist, CROXALL   109
St Peter, ELFORD   111
St Bartholomew, FAREWELL   111
St Chad, HOPWAS   112
St Chad, LICHFIELD   113
St James, LONGDON   113
All Saints, STATFOLD   114

The South-west   115
St Mary and St Chad, BREWOOD   115
St Mary, ENVILLE   116
St Peter, KINVER   118
St Mary, PATSHULL   119
St Chad, PATTINGHAM   120
All Saints, TRYSULL   121

Glossary   122

Bibliography and References   124

Index   125

Foreword

In my childhood I was aware, as most children are, of the presence of God. I would not, of course, have called it that. Yet in and through such things as the silence of a great forest near my home; through the splendour of a frosty starlit sky when we went carol singing; or through the death of my infant brother, I was somehow aware of the strange footfalls of the God of whom I was aware yet did not know.

One Easter morning, our country vicar speaking in our village church (a church not unlike some of those in this book), helped me to understand for the first time the message of the Christian faith. He explained that the God of whom I was intermittently aware has actually stepped into our world as a man in order to offer us the gift of a lasting, yet mysterious, relationship with Himself. That relationship, said our vicar, is offered to anyone who will receive it – through the reality of Jesus, Crucified and Risen.

In part, I owe that discovery to the quiet life and witness of an English village church, a building not unlike some of the fine Staffordshire churches so beautifully portrayed by Dr John Leonard in this excellent book.

My prayer is that this book may help you, dear reader, to enjoy a similar discovery. For that discovered gift leads to a lifetime's journey – into eternal life. To experience that journey is, in the end, what the Staffordshire churches – and this lovely book – are all about.

+ Keith

Acknowledgements

Many people have helped in the production of this book. Chiefly I must express my thanks to Mrs J. Morgan of Photoworld, Altrincham for her skill in developing and printing all the black-and-white photographs. I am also most grateful to the many incumbents of the various churches who have lent me their keys at unseasonable times, answered my questions, and generously given of their time and knowledge. Mr Paul Williamson, Curator of Sculpture at the Victoria and Albert Museum, has very kindly helped me with material relating to the fine statue of Christ at Swynnerton. Sir Peter Walker-Okeover and Mr Francis Wolferstan kindly gave me permission to visit and photograph All Saints Church, Okeover and All Saints Church, Statfold respectively. Mr John Wightman has very kindly read the text, and made numerous helpful suggestions and corrections. I of course am responsible for any errors that remain, and also for the opinions expressed. I must also thank Messrs Hodder and Stoughton Ltd, and Professor D.M.Palliser, for permission to reproduce the map showing parish boundaries in Needwood. It is a pleasure also to thank Mr Anton Rippon and the staff at Breedon Books for their skill in the design and technical production of this book. Finally I must thank my wife for her oft-tested patience and endurance in searching out old churches in various parts of the country, and for her invaluable help in finding many features in churches which I would otherwise have overlooked.

Introduction
Visiting Staffordshire Churches

STAFFORDSHIRE is a county which many travellers pass through but few visit. It has always been so: from the time that the Romans built Watling Street (precursor of the A5) linking London to Wroxeter and mid-Wales, travellers have gone through Staffordshire rather than to it. In the railway age, the main line from Euston to Crewe and the north-west similarly traversed the county. Today the M6 easily eclipses the A5 and the railway as the main transit route through Staffordshire. But of the millions rushing up and down the motorway, how many realise that they are skirting the edges of some beguiling countryside? And how many notice the tower of Penkridge church (Fig.1) just coming in to view in the west as they speed from Wolverhampton to Stafford?

The truth is that few people actually visit Staffordshire for pleasure. Many fail to realise that of the three-quarters of the county which lies north of Watling Street, the great majority is rural, excepting only the area around the Five Towns. The scenery is at its finest in the north, the Staffordshire Moorlands, much of which is in the Peak District National Park. But the whole of the area west of the M6 and north of Watling Street is delightful; and in the far south-west,

around Enville and Kinver, attractive rolling countryside merges into Shropshire. On the eastern side of the county, the valleys of the rivers Dove, Churnet, Tean, Blithe and Tame, tributaries all of the Trent, pass through pastoral countryside, much of which is little known. And the ancient forest of Needwood is as rich in history as in scenery.

And, of course, scattered throughout the county are the churches, nearly 100 of which are wholly or partly of medieval origin. With few exceptions, these are quite unknown outside Staffordshire. Only Clifton Campville and Ingestre (because of its possible association with Wren) are likely to be mentioned in books devoted to English parish churches.

So my expectations of finding much of value in Staffordshire were rather low: I had previously warmed to the Perpendicular churches in Cheshire, the Norman churches in Shropshire, and the Early English and Decorated churches in Derbyshire: what had Staffordshire to offer? The result confounded all my preconceived ideas, and is to be found in the pages that follow. Seventy-three lovely churches are described in some detail, and features of a few others are illustrated. Although some town churches are included (Stafford, Stone, Tamworth, Walsall, Wolverhampton), the vast

(Fig 1) **St Michael, Penkridge** *One of the fine collegiate churches of Staffordshire.*

(Fig 2) **Holy Trinity, Eccleshall** *The name 'Eccleshall' may indicate the site of a surviving Celtic Christian community.*

majority are rural, set in attractive surroundings. They have been chosen in the hope that both residents of Staffordshire and travellers through the county might be tempted to explore the wonders of these buildings so rich in architecture, history and art. And in addition to the present county, I have included some churches from the Black Country, which has historically always been part of Staffordshire, but which was transferred to the County of the West Midlands in 1974.

Which are the finest churches in Staffordshire? In addition to Clifton Campville and Ingestre, the collegiate churches (Gnosall, Penkridge, Stafford St Mary, Tamworth, Wolverhampton St Peter), together with Eccleshall (Fig.2), the seat of the bishops of Lichfield, have a good claim to the first rank.

But as well as these relatively well-known buildings, there are numerous village churches which can be even more rewarding to visit. Who has ever been to Blore, Ilam (Fig.3), Mayfield, Hamstall Ridware, Hanbury, Enville? Or to Armitage or Bradley to see the fonts, or to Swynnerton to see the Christ in Majesty? Or to Brewood or Elford to see the monuments? Or who would visit the Black Country to see St Matthew's Church, Walsall? Yet these are just a few of the delights to be found in visiting Staffordshire churches; some of those least known may have the most to offer.

In this book I have used the traditional classification of medieval churches into Norman, Early English, Decorated and Perpendicular, but perhaps a note of warning is necessary for the uninitiated. These named periods of building are the result of retrospective analysis of building styles; they did not, of course, exist in the minds of the builders. In response to changing fashion, one style merged imperceptibly into the next, usually as a result of new trends imported from the continent. And because people moved very little in the Middle Ages, it might, and often did, take 50 years for a style to spread from London and the southeast to distant counties in the north and west. So dates of specific buildings must be interpreted cautiously, for there is rarely documentary evidence of a precise date of construction.

The pleasure of visiting ancient churches is not of course confined to those who have a primarily religious interest. The history, architecture, art and craftsmanship displayed have a much broader appeal. But to those who believe, there is an added dimension of wonder and joy that the faith to which these churches bear witness is so beautifully expressed in wood and stone.

(Fig 3) **Holy Cross, Ilam** *The church is in the Manifold Valley, with Bunster Hill in the background.*

The Anglo-Saxon Church in Staffordshire

FOLLOWING the departure of the Roman legions from Britain in AD 410, the country became subject to recurring invasions of Germanic peoples – the Angles, Saxons and Jutes – who displaced the native British to the north and west. By the seventh century, the newcomers had coalesced into seven kingdoms (the Angles in Northumberland and East Anglia; the Jutes in Kent; the Saxons in Essex, Sussex and Wessex; and last to emerge, the central kingdom of Mercia, of which Staffordshire became a part. The Anglo-Saxons probably first penetrated into Staffordshire along Watling Street and the Trent valley in the early seventh century (Palliser).

Mercia was the last of the seven kingdoms formally to adopt Christianity. At the end of the sixth century (597), Pope Gregory had sent St Augustine to Kent, whence the faith gradually spread through neighbouring areas. In the north and west, pockets of Christianity persisted from Roman times, especially in those areas where the faith could be nourished by contacts with the Celtic church in Ireland. It is possible that the name 'Eccleshall' may indicate such a surviving Christian community, for the first part of the name is the Celtic word for 'church' (Greenslade and Stuart). But Mercia in general remained obdurately pagan, and for many years in the mid-seventh century it was ruled by the fierce heathen king Penda. He killed the Christian king Oswald of Northumbria in 642 and met his end at the hands of Oswald's brother Oswy in 655. Two years later Penda's son and heir Peada was baptised, and he married into the Christian Northumbrian royal family; the formal conversion of Mercia rapidly followed. Four missionary priests were sent from Northumbria to evangelise the pagan kingdom: Chad (Ceadda), Adda, Betti and Diuma. Chad, the first bishop of Mercia, was appointed in 669 by Peada's successor, Wulfhere, and fixed his see at Lichfield.

Thus Lichfield (Fig.4) appears to be the oldest

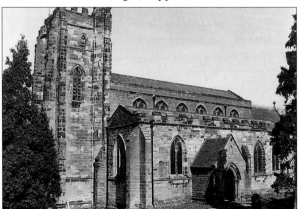

(Fig 4) **St Chad, Lichfield** *By the side of Stowe pool, St Chad's church marks the original site of St Chad's hermitage, dating back to AD 669.*

Christian site in Staffordshire (apart possibly from Eccleshall). Evidence for other Christian communities in the county in the seventh century is rather scanty: Wulfhere (king of Mercia from 659-674) is said to have founded a monastery at Stone, and his daughter, St Werburgh was an abbess of a nunnery at Hanbury, and died there in 700. An Irish abbess, St Modwen, is said to have founded a Christian community on an island in the Trent at Burton at about the same time. It is probably significant that Burton is only about five miles from Repton in Derbyshire, where a Christian community had been established by Diuma c.660.

Repton seems to have been established as the capital of Mercia in the seventh century, and became the burial place for Mercian kings. In the eighth century, Mercia became steadily more powerful, and under two successive kings (Aethelbald and Offa) it became the dominant power in the land. Offa (king from 757 to 796) established his palace at Tamworth, and in 786 the see of Lichfield was elevated to an archbishopric comprising the seven dioceses between the Thames and the Humber. But this did not last, and seven years after Offa's death in 796 Lichfield was again merged in the province of Canterbury. A cathedral chapter of a provost and nineteen prebendaries was established at Lichfield by Bishop Aethelwald in 822. After the death of Offa, Mercia went into decline, and Wessex finally emerged in the ninth century as the dominant power in Anglo-Saxon England.

The last quarter of the ninth century was marked by the Danish invasions. They had begun to harry the east coast in 787, and later steadily extended their raids, beginning to penetrate inland and to settle for the winter in various parts of eastern England. Disaster struck Mercia in 874, when the Danes spent the winter in Repton and destroyed the abbey. From this base they extended their rule, and much of Staffordshire fell under their sway. Tamworth was destroyed and St Werburgh's nunnery at Hanbury succumbed; a similar fate probably befell the monastery at Burton.

Following the sack of Repton, Alfred the Great, King of Wessex, bought peace with the Danes with money known as the Danegeld. Four years later he defeated them in battle, and negotiated a treaty restricting the Danes to the area east and north of Watling Street. The Danish region was known as the Danelaw, and two-thirds of the area which later became Staffordshire lay within it, but their hold on and influence over this region was much less than, say, in Derbyshire.

Alfred's settlement with the Danes divided Mercia into two, and the situation was highly unstable. During his reign, the remnant of Mercia became virtually a dependency of Wessex (Aethelred, King of Mercia,

(Fig 5) **St Editha, Tamworth** *Church and castle.*

married Alfred's daughter Aethelflaed, known as the Lady of the Mercians). Her brother Edward, now King of Wessex, defeated the Danes near Wednesfield in 910, and three years later Aethelflaed advanced into Danish-held areas and fortified Tamworth (Fig.5) and Stafford, the earliest recorded mention of the future county town. When Aethelflaed died at Tamworth in 918, Mercia was formally incorporated into the kingdom of Wessex, and Edward was proclaimed king of the Anglo-Saxons. He was succeeded by his son Athelstan in 924, and two years later Athelstan's sister Editha was married to the Danish king Sihtric at Tamworth; after the death of Sihtric, she is said to have governed a nunnery at Tamworth; the parish church there is dedicated to her.

Athelstan's successors more or less kept the Danes at bay until the disastrous reign of Ethelred (the Unready; 978-1016); this was followed by Danish rule over the entire country by King Canute (1016-1035). The Anglo-Saxon line was restored in the person of Edward the Confessor in 1042, and his death in 1066 opened the way to King Harold, the Battle of Hastings and the triumph of William the Conqueror.

It is not known when the shire of Stafford actually came into existence – the earliest record dates from 1016, but some authorities believe that its formation may have been as early as the end of the reign of King Edward (died 924). From Aethelflaed's time onwards, there were only two fortified towns in the shire, Stafford and Tamworth, and presumably Stafford was chosen because of its central location.

During the Anglo-Saxon centuries, it is now apparent that many more churches were founded than previously believed. Those that have survived are only a minuscule proportion of the total. The churches were nearly all built of wood, and so have perished without trace. Stone was used only for cathedrals and monasteries until *c.*950, but thereafter was used increasingly for some parish churches. But it was not until a hundred years later that large-scale stone building for local churches was undertaken.

The organisation of the church in Saxon times was relatively loose. Originally, a number of minsters arose, usually serving a very wide area, and being staffed by a variable number of canons. The early minster churches in Staffordshire certainly included Lichfield cathedral and Eccleshall; it is also likely that the group of churches which later became collegiate (p39), controlled by the king rather than the diocesan bishop, originated as minsters. In the later Saxon centuries, many village churches were founded by laymen, with only a tenuous relationship with the local bishop. These churches were often regarded by the local thane as part of his personal property, almost as a capital investment; for ownership of a church increasingly brought in revenue in the form of tithes. So the large areas originally served by the older minsters became progressively smaller as parishes multiplied.

By the time of William the Conqueror there were numerous Anglo-Saxon churches in Staffordshire – no one knows how many – but unfortunately none has survived. Only the excavated foundations of the Anglo-Saxon church of St Bertelin remain adjacent to the present church of St Mary in Stafford; this building survived until the early nineteenth century. What does remain, however, is a remarkable series of crosses dating back to Saxon times.

Anglo-Saxon Cross-shafts
Modern county boundaries have, of course, little significance for Anglo-Saxon times, so when considering Anglo-Saxon sculpture in present-day Staffordshire it is wholly artificial to ignore the leading school of Mercian sculpture which arose in the eighth century at Breedon-on-the-Hill, which is now just inside Leicestershire, though only eight miles from Repton, and the Anglo-Saxon cross-shafts which remain in neighbouring Derbyshire. At Breedon, *c.*675, a Benedictine Abbey was founded by the Mercian king Aethelred, and like Repton it was sacked by the Danes in 874. The astonishing works produced here may still be seen in the parish church of St Mary. Pevsner writes as follows: 'The sculpture is mostly in the form of friezes. They … contain geometrical ornament, Greek keys, pelta forms etc., interlace, and in addition vine or ivy scrolls.'

The vine-scroll is a Christian motif arising in the Near East and Mediterranean (Wilson), probably ultimately deriving from the fifteenth chapter of St John's Gospel ('I am the true vine'). In Anglo-Saxon sculpture it may often be difficult to recognise as a vine, and the term 'plant-scroll' is sometimes used instead. Fronded leaves and bunches of grapes may be seen, and sometimes the motif takes the form of a tree (the Tree of Life). Frequently, the plant-scrolls may be 'inhabited', featuring birds, animals, monsters and sometimes human figures. Fret and interlace patterns similar to those found in early Northumbrian manuscripts may also be seen.

Breedon flourished during the era of Mercian supremacy, that is during and shortly after the reigns of Aethelbald (726-757) and Offa (757-796). The Derbyshire sculpture which derives from the school includes the standing crosses at Bakewell, Bradbourne and Eyam. At Bakewell there are vine-scrolls and

(Fig 6) **St Peter, Wolverhampton** *The Wolverhampton pillar.*

animals, and on the west side a series of sculptures of human figures, the upper one being the Crucifixion. Across the county border into Staffordshire, similar crosses may be seen at Ilam, Leek and Checkley. Most of these crosses show prominent interlace patterns, sometimes with human figures also, and are thought to show close affinities with contemporary Anglo-Danish work in Cumberland (e.g. Gosforth, Beckermet St John).

S.A.Jeavons (b) analysed the Anglo-Saxon crossshafts in Staffordshire and found a complex situation. To the ninth century (pre-Danish) he attributes the well-known Wolverhampton pillar (Fig.6) which displays acanthus-leaf decoration deriving from the empire of Charlemagne; he was contemporary with Offa at the height of Mercian supremacy in England. Later in the ninth century, and after the arrival of the Danes, is the wheel-headed cross at Rolleston (Fig.7), said to come from Tatenhill.

In a separate category are the larger group of crossshafts in the north of the county, divided into two types by the cross-sectional shape of the shafts: (i) rectangular shafts, tapering above; and (ii) round crossshafts. The former are best seen at Ilam (Fig.8) and Checkley

(Fig 9) **St Mary, Checkley** *Another rectangular cross-shaft, with human figures and arch similar to Fig 8.*

(Fig 7) **St Mary, Rolleston** *Ninth-century wheel-headed cross, originally from Tatenhill.*

(Fig 8) **Holy Cross, Ilam** *A rectangular Anglo-Saxon cross-shaft in the churchyard. At the foot of the shaft are three human figures under a double-stranded arch.*

(Fig.9); at the foot of these crosses are a group of three human figures under a double-stranded arch. One of the crosses at Leek (Fig.10), and the cross at Stoke-on-Trent, are similar. These probably belong to the tenth century.

Later, probably early eleventh-century, are the round cross-shafts. These include the large cross at Leek (Fig.11), where the shaft is capped with a horizontal band of interlace; above this the shaft changes shape and is cut into four faces decorated with scrolls, interlace and fretwork. The cross at Chebsey, though less well-preserved, is similar (Fig.12). Across the border in Derbyshire, the cross at Brailsford has similar characteristics.

Right: (Fig 10) **St Edward the Confessor, Leek** *A further rectangular cross-shaft.*

Far right: (Fig 11) **St Edward the Confessor, Leek** *A round cross-shaft decorated above with scrolls, interlace and fretwork.*

(Fig 12) **All Saints, Chebsey** *The cross at Chebsey is similar to that at Leek.*

The Arrival of the Normans

THE victory of William the Conqueror over King Harold at the Battle of Hastings in 1066 ended Anglo-Saxon England for ever; ended also after a short time were the incessant conflicts with the Danes. But peace was bought at the price of subjugation of the people to an alien, oppressive rule; and the peasantry witnessed the appropriation of all the most valuable assets by the Norman invaders. In the north especially there was seething discontent which erupted in open rebellion in 1069-70. William's response, after crushing the uprising, was the harrying of the north – systematic pillage and despoliation of the countryside, which laid waste to vast tracts of land.

Twenty years after the Battle of Hastings, the Domesday survey was made, and reveals that Staffordshire was still bearing the scars of William's iron rule. About a fifth of the county's settlements were still described as waste, mainly in the northern uplands. The king had taken for himself large parts of the county, the other chief magnates being Roger of Montgomery, Earl of Shrewsbury, the Bishop of Chester, Robert de Stafford, William FitzAnsculf and Henry de Ferrers. Not surprisingly, much of the bishop's holdings were concentrated around Lichfield and Eccleshall. (At the time of the Domesday survey, the see had been moved from Lichfield to Chester.) There were few towns at the time of the Domesday survey: only Stafford (by far the largest), Tamworth and Tutbury could truly be described as such; each was defended by a castle.

The Normans brought with them their own style of Romanesque architecture, and in the twelfth century a comprehensive programme of church building was begun. In Staffordshire, as elsewhere, there must have been innumerable Saxon churches constructed of wood, and these of course have not survived. They were now replaced by buildings of stone on an extensive scale – it has been estimated that at least 108 churches in the county were built or rebuilt during the twelfth century (Jeavons).

In the smallest Norman churches, there was just a nave and chancel; this may be seen in its purest form in Steetley chapel in Derbyshire and Heath chapel in Shropshire. The best examples in Staffordshire of Norman building on a more substantial scale are the churches at Tutbury and Stafford (St Chad). Many Norman churches began on a small scale and then had to be enlarged to cater for the expanding population which occurred in the twelfth and thirteenth centuries. This was done by lateral extension of the nave in the form of aisles, separated from the nave by arcades of semicircular arches (Fig.13) supported by massive cylindrical piers or columns. The piers are surmounted by square-edged capitals, which effect the transition from the round column to the square abacus above which supports the arch (Fig.14). The inferior surface of the capital is often carved into a cushion (a rounding-off of the lower angles into the cylindrical shaft below), scallop (a further modification in which the surface is elaborated into a series of truncated cones) or volute (spiral scrolls).

Semicircular arches are also found above doorways and windows and are, of course, the hallmark of Norman architecture. They often became decorated by geometric designs (Fig.15), the commonest being the chevron or zigzag, which was introduced c.1120. Other Norman ornamental motifs are beak-head (the repeated use of stylised heads of birds or mammals with long beaks – Fig 25), billet (short raised rectangles placed at regular intervals) and nail-head

(Fig 14) **St John the Baptist, Mayfield** *A square Norman capital, with the inferior surface carved with scallop decoration.*

(small pyramids regularly repeated). Late in the Norman period, and continuing more typically into the next century, dog-tooth occurs (a series of four-

(Fig 13) **St Mary, Tutbury** *The massive piers of the Norman arcade.*

(Fig 15) **St James, Longdon** *Norman chancel arch with three orders of columns, with scalloped capitals.*

(Fig 16) **St Mary, High Offley** *A small round-headed Norman window, deeply splayed internally.*

cornered stars placed diagonally and raised pyramidally). Norman windows are usually small and round-headed, and are deeply splayed internally (but not externally) to maximise the provision of light, glass being expensive (Fig.16).

Norman towers are squat, sturdy, plain, solidly-built, with thick walls. At belfry level, there are usually two round-headed windows divided by a shaft, with a larger round-headed arch surmounting both.

Monastic foundations were numerous in Staffordshire: between 1000 and 1344, about 26 were established, over half of them being founded in the twelfth century, the heyday of the cloister. A few dated from before the Conquest: the Benedictines refounded Burton in 1004, Tamworth (for nuns) before 1000 and Lapley in 1061; Tutbury followed shortly afterwards in 1080. The most powerful and wealthy foundation in the county was always Burton. Lapley (a dependency of the abbey of St Remigius at Rheims) was suppressed by Henry V in 1415 because it was an alien priory, and Canwell, Farewell and Sandwell were suppressed by Cardinal Wolsey in 1525-27. The remainder perished at the Dissolution of the

Monasteries in the 1530s and passed into lay hands, though Tutbury, Stone, Trentham and part of Burton Abbey became parish churches. Monastic remains in the county are vestigial, apart from Croxden, where significant ruins survive.

St Mary, Tutbury

Tutbury – the name immediately conjures up images of Mary Queen of Scots, confined here for many a weary year. There was a royal castle at Tutbury, largely built by John of Gaunt, but by the mid-sixteenth century it was in some dilapidation. Of all Mary's many prisons, it was the one she hated most (Antonia Fraser). In winter damp and cold, with miasma rising from the marshes in the Dove valley below, it was an inhospitable and fearful place.

Today the castle, yet more ruinous, still stands imposingly above the Dove valley, and just below it is the Priory Church of St Mary the Virgin. Henry de Ferrers was the holder of Tutbury after the Norman Conquest, and the church was founded as a Benedictine priory in 1089. From the beginning it was both priory and parish church, which is just as well, or else nothing would have survived the Dissolution. What remains is the western six bays of the medieval nave – the rest, transepts, central tower, monks' choir, cloisters and monastic buildings having all crumbled into dust.

Yet even so the surviving church (Fig.17) is enormously impressive, a synthesis of Norman building and Victorian reconstruction maybe, but without the latter, how much of the former would we see now? The west front is outstanding – a Norman edifice of considerable complexity and lavish detail. The west door (Fig.18) is surrounded by an arcade of seven orders with colonettes, the capitals carved with beasts and figures, the arches with beak-head, chevron and other geometrical designs. The doorway is celebrated because in the second order above the door is the first English use of alabaster, mined locally, dated *c.*1160-70. The other orders are of gritstone. Above the door is a large semi-circular-headed window with Norman decoration around (Fig.19); the tracery of the window itself is Victorian. On either side are Norman two-light windows with blank arcading, and in the gable above three round windows with zigzag. The south doorway (Fig.20) is also Norman, with three orders of colonettes, and in the lintel above is carved a boar hunt. The rather stumpy, unimpressive tower is Perpendicular.

The interior is equally majestic. There are massive Norman piers supporting the arcades, with above a triforium now acting as a clerestory (Fig.13), and admitting much more light than is found in most Norman churches. The three westernmost piers are of an elongated quatrefoil shape, the others being cylindrical. The capitals are carved with scallops. The south aisle is Perpendicular, with windows containing most attractive stained glass by Burlison and Grylls.

(Fig 17) **The Priory Church of St Mary, Tutbury**

(Fig 18) **St Mary, Tutbury** *The west doorway.*

(Fig 19) **St Mary, Tutbury** *Windows in the west front above the doorway.*

(Fig 20) **St Mary, Tutbury** *The south doorway.*

When I visited Tutbury on a sunny day in November, the low sunshine filtering through the glass produced gorgeous dappling effects on the Norman columns. The east end of the south aisle bears the scars of the demolition work of the mid-sixteenth century. The chancel arch and apse are part of the Victorian reconstruction by Street in 1867-68.

Access: From Burton-on-Trent, take the A50 north-westwards for about five miles; in Tutbury, the A50 turns sharply right, and at this point go straight ahead into the town and the church will be found on the right, high up opposite to the castle.

St Chad, Stafford

Sited rather unobtrusively in one of the main shopping streets in Stafford is the small Norman church of St Chad, whose survival for 850 years is almost miraculous. In fact, for 200 years from 1650, dilapidation was endemic; during this time, however, the fine Norman carvings of the chancel arch and arcades were largely hidden by layers of plaster, thus preserving them for our enjoyment when St Chad's emerged from its long night of neglect in the middle of the nineteenth century. But I anticipate.

The church was founded about the middle of the twelfth century and it appears to have been built by a man called Orm; for carved on the capital of the northeast pillar of the tower is a Latin inscription translated as 'The man who established me is called Orm' (Fig. 23). Of this church, the four-bay nave arcades and clerestory survive, together with the chancel arch and the north wall at least of the chancel; most of the rest of the building dates from the restoration by Sir George Gilbert Scott in 1873-74.

From the street outside, the west front is seen to be entirely Victorian, as are the walls of the aisles; and the central tower and north transept were re-modelled in the 1880s. But step inside and the glories of twelfth-century Norman craftsmanship await you (Fig.21). The piers, of course, are sturdy, surmounted by round capitals, and above is the Norman clerestory – an unusual feature in twelfth-century churches. The church is cruciform in shape – of the crossing arches supporting the tower, the east is pointed (Norman Transitional) while the west (facing the nave) is

(Fig 22) **St Chad, Stafford** *Blank arcading of intersecting arches in the chancel.*

(Fig 23) **St Chad, Stafford** *Capital of the northeast pillar of the tower, inscribed 'Orm vocatur qui me condidit' – the man who established me is called Orm.*

(Fig 24) **St Chad, Stafford** *Grotesque carving below the capital in the north wall of the chancel.*

rounded. And it is the quality and freshness of the Norman carving on this arch which is most astonishing – the beak-head decoration (Fig.25) is so fresh that one wonders how much is due to nineteenth-century restoration. Also amazingly fresh is the intricate carving on the capitals of the demishafts of the east crossing arch. In the north and south walls of the chancel is blank arcading of intersecting arches (Figs.22, 24) – the north is genuine, the south may have been restored.

Today, St Chad's stands in the Anglo-Catholic

(Fig 21) **St Chad, Stafford** *The Norman arcade and west arch of the crossing.*

(Fig 25) **St Chad, Stafford** *Animal carvings on the south pillars of the west crossing arch.*

tradition of the Church of England – High Mass is celebrated every Sunday morning, and there is an annual pilgrimage to Our Lady of Walsingham. The focus of worship is, of course, the high altar, and behind this is a fine reredos painted by Walter Tapper in about 1910. This extends across the full width of the chancel, and includes in the centre representations of the Annunciation, the Visitation and the Nativity, with Anglo-Saxon saints (St Chad, St Werburgh, St Etheldreda, St Guthlac) in the side-panels.

Access: St Chad's is in the town centre, almost opposite the Tourist Information Centre.

The Early English Style – the Thirteenth Century

THE Early English style covers roughly the whole of the thirteenth century, and work of this period is frequently seen in Staffordshire alongside earlier Norman architecture. The reason for this is that increasing prosperity and growing population required the progressive enlargement of many churches by the addition of aisles or the lengthening of naves and chancels. Although much Norman work was sound and has stood the test of time, some was less good and required replacement. Sometimes replacement was wholesale, and preceding Saxon or Norman buildings vanished without trace, leaving us with churches which are basically Early English, with or without significant later additions. Some of the finest churches in the county come into this category – e.g. Eccleshall and St Mary, Stafford (later restored). In other cases, Early English work may be seen alongside earlier Norman building (e.g. Pattingham).

In Early English churches, the semicircular arches and thick cylindrical piers of the Norman age have

(Fig 27) **St John the Baptist, Mayfield** *Early English capital with broad-leaf carving.*

(Fig 28) **Holy Trinity, Eccleshall** *Early English capital with stiff-leaf carving.*

(Fig 26) **Holy Trinity, Eccleshall** *The interior looking east, with Early English arcades.*

(Fig 29) **St Lawrence, Coppenhall** *The interior, showing a plain Early English chancel arch and three widely separated lancet windows at the east end of the chancel.*

given way to acutely-pointed arches supported by less substantial piers (Fig.26), often with a fillet (a thin band running down the shaft). There is considerable variety in the cross-section of the piers: at first they usually remain circular, but as the century progressed octagonal or multi-shafted piers may be seen. They are now usually surmounted by capitals with a rounded (instead of a square) upper edge, and may be characteristically decorated with 'stiff-leaf' foliage (Figs.27 and 28). The dog-tooth pattern may also be found in Early English arcades. Instead of the deeply recessed small Norman windows, tall lancet windows with acutely pointed upper ends are seen (Fig.29; Fig.262, p116), often in groups of three at the east end of the chancel. Externally, lancet windows were provided with a hood-mould of projecting masonry to

throw the rain-water clear of the window. Sometimes two or more lancets were enclosed by the same hood-mould to prevent the water from puddling between them; this necessarily also enclosed a small area of blank wall at the apex below the common hood-mould. Later in the century, this area was often pierced, resulting in plate or Y-tracery above the lancet windows (Fig.30). From this germ, the later development of complex tracery seen in the next century evolved. Mayfield church has a remarkable series of windows illustrating the development of tracery in the thirteenth and fourteenth centuries (see Fig.175, p78).

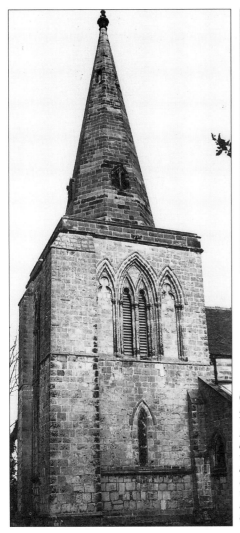

(Fig 30) **Holy Trinity, Eccleshall** *The nave looking west. Y-tracery in the west window.*

(Fig 31) **St Andrew, Weston** *Early English tower: a single lancet window below, and above twin lancet windows with blank shafted lancets on each side.*

Early English towers (Fig.31) have pointed lancet windows, and the belfry windows become more prominent. Spires were sometimes built in the thirteenth century – usually broach spires in which semi-pyramidal pieces of masonry at the top of the tower effected a smooth transition to the octagonal spire; these are rare in Staffordshire. Buttresses in the thirteenth century were usually placed at each corner, at right-angles to each other. The projection of the buttresses diminishes towards the top of the tower, and was reduced stepwise with a sloping set-off to shed rainwater.

St Lawrence, Coppenhall

Here is a building for purists who like their churches to be of one style: for St Lawrence's, though small, is a virtually unaltered church of the thirteenth century, and so is a classic example of the Early English period. In those days it was a dependency of the collegiate church at Penkridge, and later was described as a chapel-of-ease to Penkridge.

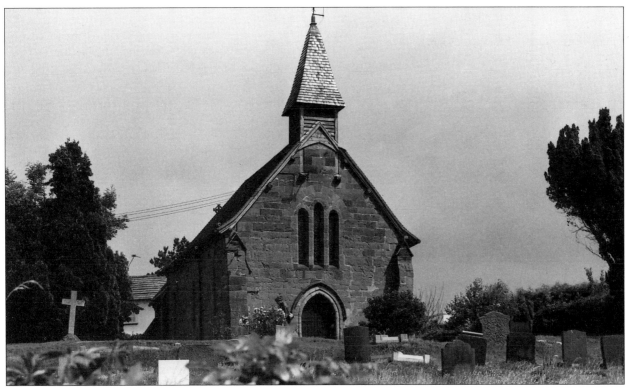

(Fig 32) **St Lawrence, Coppenhall** *A small Early English church.*

(Fig 33) **Holy Trinity, Eccleshall** *Early English piscina and sedilia.*

It stands prominently on a bluff (Fig.32), exposed to the west winds, and can look bleak and austere in poor weather. Constructed of stone, it consists only of nave and chancel, with a Victorian bell-turret and spirelet at the west end. The interior is plain and rather dark. In the west wall are three lancet windows contained internally under a single arch above the west doorway. There are further lancet windows, some renewed, along both north and south walls of the nave and the south wall of the chancel. The east wall has three widely spaced lancets, with a Victorian round window above (Fig.29). The chancel arch is simple and springs from semicircular responds.

Access: From junction 13 of the M6 south of Stafford, go for about a third of a mile along the A449 towards Penkridge, and then turn right just before Dunston; after half a mile, turn right again, and at the next crossroads, right yet again for Coppenhall. In the village, turn left, and the church is on the left-hand side. The key may usually be obtained at one of the neighbouring cottages.

Holy Trinity, Eccleshall

Situated in unspoilt countryside towards the Shropshire border, Eccleshall, with its fine High Street, ancient castle (not open to the public) and magnificent parish church (Fig.2, p8) is a place to visit. It is a very ancient settlement, said to have received its name (meaning 'church in a hollow') in

Anglo-Saxon times (Gelling). Domesday Book states that Eccleshall was owned by the Bishop of Chester (the see of Lichfield had been transferred to Chester in 1075, twelve years before Domesday). By the time of that survey, however, the cathedral clergy had long owned large estates around Eccleshall, extending from just outside Stafford to the Shropshire border. It has been argued that, because of the first element in the place-name, this was a minster estate possibly based on a pre-existing Celtic Christian community, and that the original beneficiary might well have been St Chad himself or one of his successors (Palliser).

In 1102, the see was moved from Chester to Coventry and remained there until the Reformation. The diocese therefore had three major centres – Chester, Coventry and Lichfield – and it is perhaps understandable that the bishops should choose Eccleshall as their residence; although small, it was at least geographically more central than the larger towns. Whatever the reason, the bishops of Coventry and Lichfield (as they were styled) resided in Eccleshall Castle from the thirteenth to the nineteenth centuries. This may explain why Eccleshall was blessed with such a large and impressive church, in which six bishops of the diocese are buried.

Approaching the church from the road, notice first the south wall of the chancel, with its series of Early English lancet windows. The lower part of the tower (Fig.2), is also Early English – below the clock are two windows with grouped lancets under a common hood-mould. The windows of the south aisle are similar. The

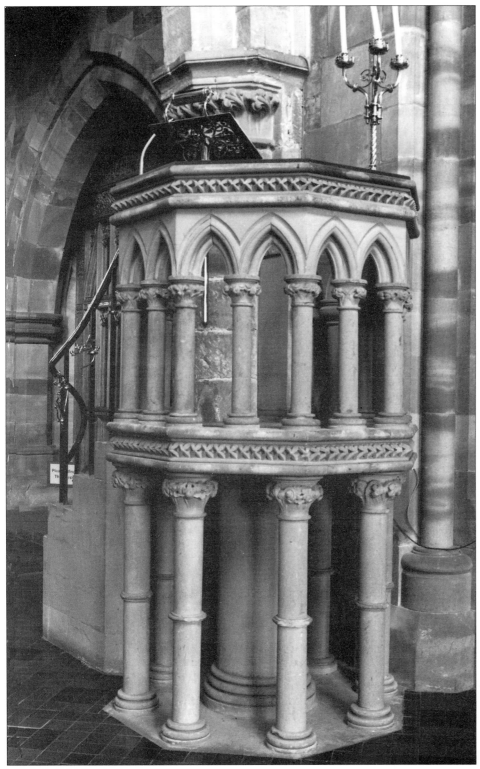

(Fig 34) **Holy Trinity, Eccleshall** *The Victorian stone pulpit.*

The interior has fine Early English arcades (Figs.26 and 30) supported by round piers with stiff-leaf carving on the capitals (Fig.28). The lancets in the east wall of the chancel date from the Victorian restoration. The simple font made of red sandstone is of the thirteenth century.

To the north of the chancel is the Lady Chapel, furnished in memory of Mary Lowe, who died of meningitis in 1927, just before her twenty first birthday. The architect W.D.Caröe designed the lovely limed oak carving, which was executed by the Lichfield firm of Bridgemans.

Even more rewarding is the chancel itself: in the south wall are the elegant Early English piscina and sedilia (Fig. 33), and next to this is the bishop's throne. Behind the high altar is a very fine reredos constructed of Staffordshire alabaster in 1892. The stone pulpit (Fig.34) is also Victorian. In the north wall of the chancel is the finest monument in the church – that to Bishop Overton, who died in 1609; his effigy is shown recumbent on the tomb-chest, and behind and above him are his two wives, kneeling (Fig.122, p60.).

tower was heightened in the fifteenth century in the Perpendicular style, with the two-light bell-windows under a single ogee arch, surmounted by a decorative frieze, gargoyles and battlements; the pinnacles are Victorian. The clerestory, with its fine array of windows, is also typically Perpendicular.

Access: From junction 15 of the M6, take the A519 southwards for Eccleshall; from junction 14, take the A5013 westwards. The church is on the western border of the town, on the right-hand side of the B506 which leads to Ashley Heath and Market Drayton.

The Decorated Style – the Fourteenth Century

THE Decorated style was introduced elsewhere in England around 1300, and arrived in Staffordshire somewhat later; the two great Decorated churches of the county are Clifton Campville and Tamworth. Decorated arches are not so acutely pointed as in the preceding period, and the piers are more often octagonal or multi-shafted than circular in cross-section (Fig.42, p25; Fig.81, p45). The carvings on the moulded capitals are freer and more elaborate, and when foliage is seen it is more realistic than the stiff-leaf carving of the Early English style. Around 1300 or shortly after, a development of the Y-tracery seen in the later part of the Early English period occurred in which each mullion of grouped lancets of the window branched out into two curved bars, forming so-called intersecting tracery (Figs. 35 and 36; also Figs.193, p85 and 235, p103.).

But the most characteristic feature of the Decorated style, which was to stamp its hallmark on the whole fourteenth century, was the ogee-arch – two shallow S-shaped curves meeting upwards in a sharp point, and often embellished with crockets and other ornamental features. There was nothing functional about the ogee arch – it was an exuberant artistic fancy. In windows it led to complicated patterns of flowing tracery (Figs. 37 and 38; also Figs. 15, p14, 175, p78 and 220, p96),

(Fig 36) **St Andrew, Clifton Campville** *An early form of Decorated window tracery.*

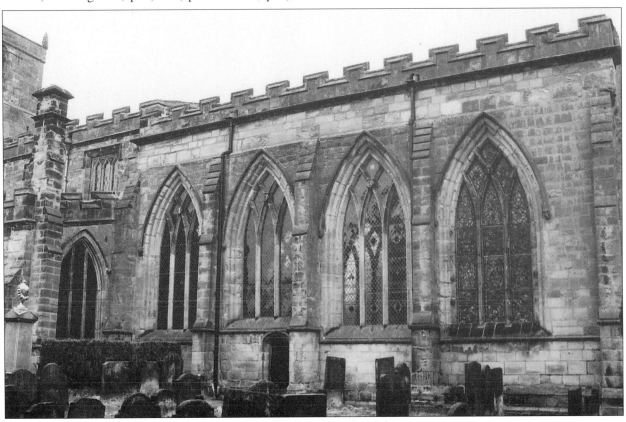

(Fig 35) **St Mary, Checkley** *Intersecting window tracery.*

22

(Fig 37) **St Andrew, Clifton Campville** *More complex Decorated window tracery.*

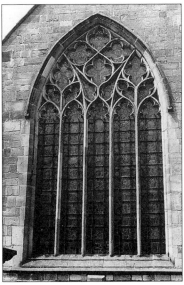

(Fig 38) **St Laurence, Gnosall** *Complex flowing tracery.*

(Fig 39) **St Mary, Rolleston** *Decorated tower and recessed spire.*

some of which may be described as geometrical, curvilinear or reticulated. Another characteristic motif of the Decorated age was ball-flower ornamentation – a small ball enclosed by three petals forming a globular flower; this was often set in rows on a concave moulding on windows and elsewhere (Fig. 166, p75).

Decorated towers were typically of four storeys: the ground floor, opening into the nave through the tower arch; above this, a ringers' gallery, with small windows; then the belfry, with prominent windows; and at the top, the roof surmounted with a spire, usually recessed within a parapet (Figs.39, 40). Buttressing in the fourteenth and later centuries was usually diagonal, placed at the four corners of the structure.

St Andrew, Clifton Campville

The finest medieval parish church in Staffordshire (Fig.40) is situated in the extreme east of the county, close to the border with Leicestershire. If it were in Suffolk, it could be ranked with Lavenham or Long Melford and everyone would have heard of it. But its location in an obscure corner of an obscure county ensures that outside Staffordshire it is almost entirely unknown.

Clifton is mentioned in Domesday Book, but the second element of the village name does not appear until the thirteenth century, Campville being a family name of Norman origin. At the time of the Domesday survey, the area around Clifton was among the most prosperous in the county.

The earliest part of the church is the two-storeyed north transept (Fig.41): the ground floor is an exquisitely vaulted chapel, recently refurnished, and

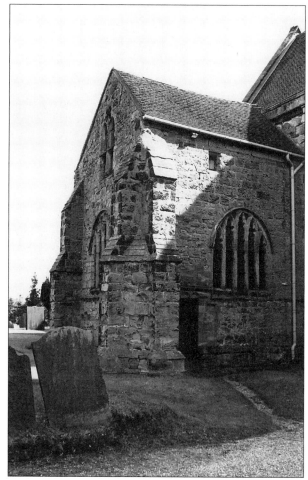

(Fig 41) **St Andrew, Clifton Campville** *The two-storeyed north transept.*

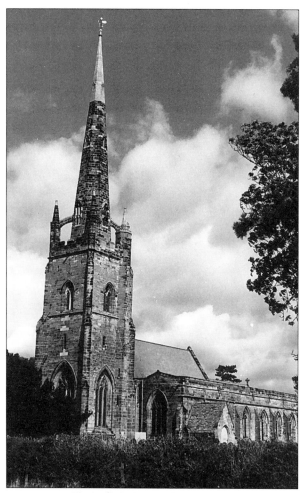

(Fig 40) **St Andrew, Clifton Campville**

above is a priest's chamber. There are stepped lancet windows to the north and west, indicating a date towards the end of the Early English period (*c.*1300).

From early in the eighteenth century, the transept served as the chapel of the Pye family whose monuments by Rysbrack are in the chancel. Of the same period as the north transept is the chancel, which is spacious and has one lancet window. The whole of the rest of the church is Decorated, dating from the first half of the fourteenth century.

Externally, the tower with pinnacles, and spire supported by flying buttresses, make a fine impression, and the interior fully lives up to expectations. The church consists of the tower, the nave with the north transept, chancel with south chapel, and a south aisle. The lofty windows in the tower flood the church with light. The arcade (Fig.42) separating the south aisle from the nave, and that separating the chancel from the south chapel, are both quatrefoil in cross-section. The windows of the south aisle are Decorated in style (Figs.36, 37), and Decorated windows are inserted into Early English walls in the east wall of the chancel and north side of the nave.

The three medieval screens are described and illustrated on pp64-65, Fig. 138. In the chancel are choir-stalls with misericords dating from the fourteenth century. In the south chapel is a fine alabaster monument to Sir John Vernon and his wife (1545); their effigies lie in conventional repose, while against the sides of the tomb-chest are kneeling children, bedesmen, and shields with supporters (Fig. 110, p57). In the chancel, note the monuments to the Pye family

by Rysbrack, dated 1736.

    Access: From Tamworth, take the A513 north for four miles, and then turn right towards Harlaston; at the T-junction, turn left, pass through Harlaston and Haunton to Clifton Campville. The church is along a short lane on the right.

(Fig 42) **St Andrew, Clifton Campville** *Decorated south arcade, with columns quatrefoil in cross-section.*

The Perpendicular Style –
1350-1550

BUBONIC plague struck England in 1348-1350, and the Black Death wiped out a quarter, perhaps a third, of the population. It is a tribute to the faith in medieval times that, in this ghastly fourteenth century, when plague was compounded by bad harvests and disaster occurred on a scale never known in England before or since, there was no pause in church building in many counties. In Cheshire, for example, there was a notable surge of building between 1350 and 1400, and later, in the fifteenth

(Fig 44) **St Michael, Tatenhill** *Straight-headed 'Tudor' nave window.*

later styles, and St Peter's is atypical for Staffordshire.

The reason for the relative dearth of Perpendicular building must, I think, lie in the economic circumstances of the county during the fifteenth century. At a time when there was great prosperity in other parts of the country, for example East Anglia, and Perpendicular churches were constructed on the most ambitious scale, Staffordshire remained relatively poor, and probably the population failed to grow after the Black Death. So, with few exceptions, all that was

needed, or could be afforded, was relatively small-scale amendments to the existing buildings.

Towers were often heightened, and received battlements and pinnacles (Fig.43; Fig. 161, p72). The steeply sloping roofs of earlier centuries were replaced by low-pitched roofs (Fig.173, p77); this enabled the side walls of the naves to be heightened, thus allowing for the insertion of a clerestory, which now became the rule for parish churches and brought a welcome increase in light. Perpendicular windows, often the straight-headed variety known as Tudor windows (Fig.44), were frequently inserted into the walls of naves, aisles and chancels of previous buildings.

The Perpendicular style prevailed in England for 200 years (*c.*1350-1550), persisting until the Reformation. The emphasis throughout is on verticality; straight lines replace the sinuous tracery of

(Fig 43) **St Michael, Horton** *Perpendicular tower, with battlements and pinnacles.*

century, all the noblest medieval churches in the county were completed (Nantwich, Bunbury, Astbury, Malpas, Great Budworth). In Staffordshire, however, although Perpendicular work may be seen in many buildings, only Barton-under-Needwood is built entirely in the Perpendicular style. On a much grander scale is the collegiate church of St Peter, Wolverhampton, built with the wealth which came from wool and other merchandise in the fifteenth century; but there is significant building in earlier and

(Fig 45) **St Editha, Church Eaton** *Early English north arcade; Perpendicular east window.*

the Decorated period; the pointed arches become flatter. This 'alters the proportions of the arcade: a larger part of its height is now taken up by the piers. The piers being both taller and thinner make the arcade appear loftier (Fig.86, p48) and produce the impression of height and lightness of structure that is so characteristic of the Perpendicular style … The preference for straight lines shows particularly clearly in window tracery. There the vertical mullions that divide a window into its lights rise almost without

(Fig 46) **St James, Barton-under-Needwood**

interruption to the head of the window (Fig.45), ruling its tracery into tiers of rectangular compartments.' (Foster).

St James, Barton-under-Needwood

The name 'Barton' is thought in most instances to mean 'outlying grange' (Ekwall), and this would fit with Barton-under-Needwood, which was originally

an outlying settlement in the parish of Tatenhill, being first mentioned in 941 when King Edmund made a grant of lands in the area. At the time of Domesday Book, the manor was held by the king; later it was granted to Henry de Ferrers, but reverted to the Crown in the thirteenth century, continuing with other estates in the Duchy of Lancaster.

In the Middle Ages, Barton was a chapel-of-ease in

(Fig 47) **St James, Barton-under-Needwood** *The nave, looking west towards the high tower arch.*

(Fig 48) **St James, Barton-under-Needwood** *The arcades.*

the parish of Tatenhill, the first record of this being in 1157. No trace of this building remains; it was replaced in the early sixteenth century by the present church. This is a remarkable building, because it was built *in toto* by one man, John Taylor, between the years 1517 and 1533. This gives it an architectural unity rare in English parish churches.

John Taylor was one of triplets born in Barton during the reign of Henry VII. This being thought a remarkable event in those days of high infant mortality, the boys were shown to the king when he was hunting in Needwood Forest, and he undertook to provide for their education. Subsequently, John Taylor

rose to great heights in the next reign, being one of the chaplains who attended Henry VIII at the meeting with François I, King of France, at the Field of the Cloth of Gold. Later he acted as one of Henry's ambassadors abroad, and was appointed Master of the Rolls in 1527.

So Barton church (Fig.46) is late Perpendicular, being built just at the time of the Reformation. It is idle to pretend that it can rival the great Perpendicular churches of other parts of the country – of the Cotswolds, or East Anglia, for example – but it is none the less a fine building for what was still only a chapel-of-ease (it did not become a parish in its own right until 1881). The church is battlemented throughout, the short tower replete with eight pinnacles. The tower arch is high (Fig.47) and the arcades consist of five bays, the piers being octagonal (Fig.48); on the spandrels of the arcades are references in Latin to John Taylor alternating with his coat of arms. The chancel is most unusual as it has a three-sided apse, rare in this country but much commoner on the continent. The east window was reconstructed in Victorian times, but still contains some Tudor glass, notably in the figure of Mary in the crucifixion scene. The oldest object in the church is the medieval chest from the former church, built of wood from Needwood Forest.

Access: Barton-under-Needwood is 1 mile west from the A38, a little nearer to Burton upon Trent than to Lichfield. From Burton, proceed south for about four miles, and then B5016 leads westwards to the village, the church being on the left.

The Seventeenth Century

THE age of religious strife did not leave Staffordshire unscathed. In the reign of Mary I (1553-58), seven Protestant 'heretics' were burnt in the diocese of Lichfield. After the accession of Elizabeth I, the new religious settlement was generally accepted in London and the south-east; but elsewhere in the country the old faith was maintained for a while with varying degrees of success. In Staffordshire and Derbyshire in particular Catholicism retained the allegiance of a substantial proportion of the aristocracy. After the papal ex communication of Elizabeth in 1570 (which declared her Catholic subjects free of allegiance to her), tension heightened and the persecution of Catholics was intensified. Some of the old Staffordshire families were noted recusants: the Giffards of Chillington, for instance, remained Catholics for three hundred years after the Reformation. Their influence ensured that most of the tenants on their estate were Catholics, and that Wolverhampton remained the strongest Catholic centre in the county (Greenslade and Stuart). Similar protection by the aristocracy operated at Swynnerton, where the Fitzherberts have remained Catholics until the present day. There is no doubt that the presence of Mary Queen of Scots in the neighbourhood acted as a magnet and focus of allegiance to a number of the local gentry: after the discovery of the Babington plot and the execution of the Queen, priests hidden in Catholic houses were hunted down and one, Robert Sutton, was executed in Stafford in 1588.

After the Reformation, church building in Staffordshire, as elsewhere in England, came virtually to a halt, and during the next 150 years was mainly limited to repair work and essential maintenance. There were, however, some exceptions, and in the early seventeenth century there was building in the Perpendicular style at Betley, Caverswall, Checkley, Ilam, Maer and Rushton Spencer. Two outstanding new churches were built in this century: at Broughton in 1630 and at Ingestre in 1676. The former looks back to the Perpendicular age; the latter looks forward to the eighteenth century, and is probably the most famous of all parish churches in Staffordshire.

St Peter, Broughton

Broughton was in the hands of the Broughton family from the thirteenth century to 1914, and their handsome hall (now a Franciscan convent) opposite

(Fig 49) **St Peter, Broughton**

(Fig 50) **St Peter, Broughton** *The interior, complete with box-pews.*

(Fig 51) **St Peter, Broughton** *The cartouche of William Bagot (1687)*

the church is one of the finest half-timbered houses in Staffordshire. The hall is dated 1637, and was one of the last timbered halls; the church was also built in a very conservative fashion by Thomas Broughton as a private chapel about seven years earlier, replacing a previous building. Architecturally, both hall and church look back to the styles of the previous century and before, and one looks in vain for evidence of classical influence. Originally it is thought that St Peter's was used only by the Broughtons, but from 1711 local gentry agreed to worship there by permission of Sir Brian Broughton. There is no village

of Broughton (Palliser refers to it as 'a deserted settlement'), and the church stands alone, just to the west of the main road (Fig.49). Externally, the building is plain, in the so-called debased Perpendicular style of the early seventeenth century; but it is not unattractive, and the surrounding churchyard is well-maintained.

But inside, St Peter's, is outstanding, preserving a fine seventeenth-century interior with a complete set of high-walled box-pews (Fig.50). Monuments abound to the Broughton family, and to the Delves family from nearby Doddington Hall in Cheshire, the two families being joined in marriage in 1727. Stained glass of high quality has been brought from elsewhere; in the south window of the chancel is Sir John Delves, slain at the battle of Tewkesbury (1471) and his wife; in the east window are figures of saints – the figures of St George and St Roche have been identified as originating in the workshop of Robert Power at Burton upon Trent, *c.*1500 (Marks). There is an unique font set in a carved recess in a tower pier; this is thought to be probably a pre-Reformation holy water stoup, and might possibly be of Roman origin. Monuments to the Broughtons abound, including cartouches of William Bagot (1687; Fig. 51) and Spencer Broughton (1702-03). In the north window of the chancel is some heraldic glass.

Access: Broughton is on the B5026, from Eccleshall to Ashley Heath, half-a-mile beyond Wetwood, standing alone on the left side of the road. The key may be obtained from the vicarage at Wetwood.

St Mary, Ingestre

Ingestre is an ancient settlement, named in Domesday Book as Gestreon. The Chetwynd family settled here in the Middle Ages, Walter Chetwynd being member of parliament for Stafford in 1491 – a pattern of representation which recurred frequently in the next 300 years. A later Walter Chetwynd built Ingestre Hall in 1638, and a third Walter initiated the rebuilding of the church in 1676, the medieval church having become ruinous. Walter was a friend of Sir Christopher Wren, and both were members of the Royal Society; at the time Wren was president, Robert Plot, who wrote the 'Natural History of Staffordshire' containing a description of the new church at Ingestre, was secretary. So although there is no written proof that Wren designed St Mary's, the links are obviously close; and the internal architectural evidence is compelling.

For this is the finest seventeenth-century church outside London. It stands close to the hall, and consists of a western tower, an aisled nave and a long chancel. The tower (Fig.52) has a west doorway, with Tuscan columns at each side and above a pediment. This in turn is surmounted by a garlanded shield and clock; and at the top, an urned balustrade. The arched windows of the aisles and the circular windows of the clerestory admit plenty of light on a sunny day, and

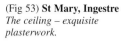

(Fig 53) **St Mary, Ingestre**
The ceiling – exquisite plasterwork.

Left: (Fig 52) **St Mary, Ingestre**

Below: (Fig 54) **St Mary, Ingestre** *The north arcade of columns with clustered shafts, looking east.*

illuminate the exquisite plasterwork of the ceiling (Fig.53) – one of the finest ceilings in any English parish church. The aisles are separated from the nave by an arcade of columns with clustered shafts (Figs. 54, 55). The tripartite screen of Flemish oak is finely carved and above is the Royal arms carved by Grinling Gibbons. To the south is the pulpit, with its tester above. The chancel ceiling is a plaster tunnel-vault. Memorials to the Chetwynds, and their successors, the Talbots, abound, but none is outstanding.

Access: From Stafford, take the A518 north-eastwards to Weston, and turn right on to the A51. After one mile, turn right into a poorly-surfaced road which crosses the Trent; after half-a-mile at a T-junction turn left, then right again for Ingestre. The church is on the right, the hall (whence the key may be obtained) is on the left.

Below: (Fig 55) **St Mary, Ingestre** *The north arcade, looking west.*

The Eighteenth Century

A CYNIC might say that the age of religious strife was followed by an age of apathy. Certainly, once the Protestant Succession was secured by the Glorious Revolution of 1688, the heat was taken out of the religious issue, and a new era of Enlightenment began, bringing with it an increasing degree of toleration. In some areas the Church of England became somewhat somnolent, till roused by one of its more turbulent priests, John Wesley. Pockets of Catholicism persisted in several parts of Staffordshire, but the religious animosity of earlier years was steadily waning. Indeed, when the new Anglican church of St John, Wolverhampton was being built, the local Catholics were eager to contribute to the costs, partly, perhaps, as an insurance policy in case 'troublesome times should come again' (Greenfield and Stuart).

There was extensive building and rebuilding of parish churches in the eighteenth century: Pevsner lists over thirty, and notes that many of them were in towns. But village churches were also built (e.g. Bradley-in-the-Moors, Marchington, Waterfall), and notable estate churches include Patshull and Weston-under-Lizard. Many of the village churches were only partially rebuilt: for example, Shareshill, Forton and Mavesyn Ridware retain their medieval towers, while Farewell has a medieval chancel.

After the Reformation, the centrepiece for worship had to some extent been moved from the altar to the pulpit, and that classic of eighteenth-century worship, the three-decker pulpit, evolved to meet this need. The lowest level was reserved for the clerk who led the congregational responses; from the intermediate level, the priest conducted the service; and then he ascended to the top level to deliver the lengthy sermon. Above the top deck, a sounding-board or tester provided the necessary resonance.

So Georgian churches were essentially for preaching, and the interiors were usually plain rect-angular boxes, the larger ones generously provided with galleries. In Staffordshire, St Michael, Stone, St John, Wolverhampton, and St Modwen, Burton upon Trent are elegant examples of the eighteenth century at its best.

St John, Wolverhampton

By the middle of the eighteenth century, the growth of Wolverhampton had outstripped the capacity of St Peter's, in spite of the creation of chapels-of-ease at Wednesfield, Willenhall and Bilston. A new building became necessary, and so in the late 1750s St John's was built to the west of the town centre. Contributions

(Fig 56) **St John, Wolverhampton**

to the building fund included donations from the local Roman Catholic community (always significant in Wolverhampton); they 'depended on their Protestant neighbours for trade and also because 'if troublesome times should come again 'twill keep the mob from molesting our chapel' (Greenslade and Stuart) – a reference to the disturbances in the town following the Glorious Revolution of 1688. It appears that the architect of the new building was William Baker of Audlem, who had succeeded James Gibbs at Patshull, and the builder was Roger Eykin.

St John's now stands in its square (Fig.56), but its environment has suffered by the construction of the ring road nearby. Nevertheless it remains a graceful building, with a fine tower, surmounted by an octagonal bell-stage and a spire. The influence of Gibbs, who designed All Saints, Derby (now the cathedral) and St Martin-in-the-Fields, London, (as well as St Mary, Patshull nearby), is said to be apparent in the design of the tower and the side windows. The church is built of brick, covered with stone ashlar.

The interior (Fig.57) is a typical Georgian church, with galleries on three sides. The western gallery

(Fig 57) **St John, Wolverhampton** *The elegant Georgian interior.*

(Fig 59) **St Luke, Shareshill** *The arched screen separating the chancel from the nave.*

displays a fine Royal Arms of George III, carved in wood and gilded. Behind the altar is a late eighteenth-century painting by Joseph Burney, a copy of Rubens' Deposition, the original being in Antwerp Cathedral. There are some notable stained-glass windows, especially in the north aisle and in the Kilby chapel to the north of the chancel.

Access: St John's is a short walk westwards from the town centre.

St Luke, Shareshill

Shareshill is an attractive village that is really an outer suburb of Wolverhampton. St Luke's is half-medieval and half-eighteenth-century, having a Perpendicular tower and a Georgian nave and chancel. The tower is late Perpendicular – sixteenth century, though the base is said to be older – and as so often with Perpendicular towers there is a decorative frieze of saltire crosses below the battlements.

The body of the church is attractive both inside and out. Externally, the most prominent feature is the semicircular porch resting on two pairs of Tuscan columns (Fig.58). The windows of the nave are tall and round-headed, and on the south side each window is surmounted by balustrading in the parapet. The east end of the church is a semicircular apse with a Venetian window.

The interior is dominated by a lovely screen of three arches supported by two columns (Fig.59) which separate the apse from the nave. The ceiling of the apse is a half-vault, and that of the nave is coved (Fig.60). Both are beautiful examples of the period. On the south side of the nave are the Royal Arms of George I. Many of the original furnishings survive, though they are rather plain – pulpit, communion rail, box-pews and west gallery. Two defaced alabaster effigies to Sir Humphrey Swynnerton and his wife (1560) lie on the window-sills, the tomb chest on which they previously rested not having survived.

Access: From Junction 11 of the M6, proceed south along A460 towards Wolverhampton; after ½ mile, turn right for Shareshill. In the village, turn left and the church is on the right.

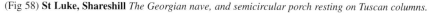

(Fig 58) **St Luke, Shareshill** *The Georgian nave, and semicircular porch resting on Tuscan columns.*

(Fig 60) **St Luke, Shareshill** *Ceiling of the nave.*

The Nineteenth and Twentieth Centuries

THE RAPID growth of population following the Industrial Revolution necessitated extensive building and rebuilding of churches in the nineteenth century; in addition, many medieval churches were showing the effects of age, and much restoration work was performed, some of which was excessive and insensitive by today's standards. It is not possible in a work of this scale to describe more than a handful of nineteenth-century churches in Staffordshire, and I have not attempted to review Nonconformist or Catholic buildings.

In the first thirty years of the nineteenth century, classical styles remained in favour, and many urban churches were built by a Commission established by the Church Building Act of 1818 in an effort to cope with rising populations. Many of these buildings were undistinguished. But during these years before the Gothic Revival (largely initiated by Pugin), some churches of value were built or re-modelled, and in Staffordshire quite the best is St Matthew, Walsall, rebuilt in 1820-21 by Francis Goodwin.

But the Gothic Revival did not burst unheralded on an unsuspecting public in 1835 (the year of Pugin's conversion to Catholicism). From the middle of the eighteenth century, choice spirits such as Thomas Gray (of the famous Elegy) and Horace Walpole were growing dissatisfied with classical forms, and were beginning to regard medieval architecture with greater enthusiasm than their contemporaries. In 1817, Thomas Rickman published his 'Attempt to Discriminate the Styles of English Architecture', which for the first time analysed medieval buildings in terms which, though perhaps not ideal, have stood the test of time and have survived until the present day. As a result of this, architects began consciously to look back to medieval styles, now formally described as Norman, Early English, Decorated or Perpendicular; and under the remarkable influence of Pugin, a revolution in taste was rapidly accomplished.

Another important development within the established church was the launching of the Oxford movement (the Tractarians) following a sermon preached by John Keble in 1833. 'The Tractarians . . arrived at Gothic architecture by reversing Pugin's position. He had said: To revive Gothic architecture you must also revive old forms of worship. They said: To revive old forms of worship you must revive Gothic architecture. His impulse had been primarily architectural, theirs was primarily religious.' (Kenneth Clark).

There are innumerable Victorian churches in Staffordshire of the Gothic Revival, including of course Pugin's great Catholic church at Cheadle. I have chosen two representative ones of the 1840s: Armitage (p108) is unusual for it is neo-Norman and not strictly neo-Gothic, and Leigh (p86) is perfect, as a nineteenth-century building in the Decorated style of five hundred years previously. Later in the century Street designed Denstone (1860-62), and Bodley the superb Hoar Cross (1872-76); both (but especially Hoar Cross) reflect the increasing Anglo-Catholic influence in the Church of England. Other Victorian churches which are described later include Ashley, Elford and Hopwas.

In the twentieth century, churches of all denominations abound in Staffordshire, but with the exception of the collegiate church at Tettenhall (rebuilt after being destroyed by fire in the 1950s) I have felt these to be outside the scope of this survey.

St Matthew, Walsall

The church of St Matthew (Fig.62) sails, gleaming white, above the town of Walsall like a ship of the line, proudly asserting its dominance over the flotilla of shops and markets and houses huddled below. The analogy is not altogether fanciful, because the medieval nave and tower were indeed encased in Bath

(Fig 61) **St Matthew, Walsall** *The nave and ceiling.*

stone in 1820, leaving just the chancel with its original sandstone masonry. The former windows were bricked up and replaced by larger ones with cast-iron tracery in the Perpendicular style.

(Fig 62) **St Matthew, Walsall**

The interior is light and airy, with thin Perpendicular arcades again of cast-iron, the nave being surrounded by galleries on three sides. The lovely ceiling (Fig.61) is of moulded plaster resembling fan-vaulting, with pendants. There is an octagonal font of the fifteenth century and nearby the deformed effigy of Sir Roger Hillary (died 1399).

The chancel is much darker than the nave, and houses a piscina and sedilia to the south of the altar and a stone lectern on the north wall. The fine set of choir-stalls, with bench-ends (Fig.157, p70), poppyheads, and eighteen misericords dating from the fifteenth century are outstanding. The misericords (Fig.156, p70), all different, include several masks, a pelican, a centaur, a miller carrying a sack, and various beasts and tree-foliage.

Access: St Matthew's is just to the east of the town centre. It is possible to park next door to the church, or alternatively, park in the town centre, and walk up through the market and then up a steep flight of steps.

All Saints, Denstone

Denstone, in the lower Churnet Valley, although mentioned in the Domesday Book, remained a small settlement for centuries, and had no church of its own until the mid-nineteenth century. Then Sir Percival Heywood, who lived nearby at Doveleys, commissioned an architect to design a church, vicarage and school, and Denstone was constituted a

(Fig 64) **All Saints, Denstone** *The east end of the chancel*

parish. The architect was G.E.Street, who certainly composed a distinguished series of buildings. All Saints was built in 1860-62 of local stone; and it was designed deliberately to express the Anglo-Catholic revival of the day within the Church of England. Yet it is not oppressive in its highchurchmanship – as perhaps some may think Hoar Cross is. Street designed not only the building, but was also responsible for the smallest details of the interior, giving the church an architectural unity. Thus the font, pulpit, low stone screen, reredos, choir stalls and organ casing make an impressive grouping.

From the approach through the churchyard on the

(Fig 63) **All Saints, Denstone**

(Fig 65) **All Saints, Denstone** *The ornate pulpit.*

south (Fig.63), the most arresting feature is the series of unusual windows on the south side of the nave – three windows, all of different design, contrasting sharply with the simple lancets in the north wall. The chancel is substantially higher than the nave and has a rounded apsidal east end (Fig.64). The rather small tower is tucked away behind the building.

The church is not large, and the furnishing with chairs rather than with pews enhances its suitability for modern worship. The focus of interest is intentionally of course the chancel, which is set at a higher level than the nave, and is well lit by large windows with plate tracery. The internal decor is rich but satisfying, the ornate pulpit (Fig.65) being perhaps a good example of Street's interior design; only the font might be regarded by some as rather too exuberant.

Access: From Uttoxeter, take B5030 northwards, and just after the JCB works at Rocester, turn left into B5031. All Saints' church is on the left after about ¾ of a mile.

The Church of the Holy Angels, Hoar Cross

It is conjectured that the settlement of Hoar Cross, on the old boundary between the parishes of Hanbury and Yoxall, may preserve the memory of an ancient boundary cross (Pallister) – see map on p100; the name is first recorded in Pipe Rolls of 1230. After the Norman Conquest, Needwood Chase became the hunting preserve of the Ferrers, and Hoar Cross was one of the grants of land which they made for colonisation in the thirteenth century. In 1399, ownership of the chase passed to the crown, and by the reign of Henry VI (1422-61) the Welles family owned a manor house here, with a small chapel. By the eighteenth century, the estate was in the hands of the Talbots, Earls of Shrewsbury, but in 1794 it was acquired by the Meynells.

The present church was built in memory of Hugo Francis Meynell Ingram, who had died in 1871, by his widow. The hall next to the church had just been completed by the time of her husband's death. The architect was J.F.Bodley, one of the greatest of the late Victorian architects, and Hoar Cross ranks with Pendlebury, Lancashire, and Eccleston, Cheshire, as his finest achievements; later, he designed the church of St Chad, Burton upon Trent (Fig.68). Hoar Cross is *the* Victorian church to see in Staffordshire – and

(Fig 66) **Holy Angels, Hoar Cross**

(Fig 67) **Holy Angels, Hoar Cross** *The altar and reredos.*

(Fig 68) **St Chad, Burton upon Trent**

indeed must rank among the top dozen nineteenth-century churches anywhere in the country.

Externally the building impresses by its sheer size and dominating position on high ground overlooking the valley of the River Swarbourn. The cruciform church, with its tall, central tower (Fig. 66), raises expectations that are not disappointed when one steps inside. Then, even on a sunny day, the dimness is all-enveloping; but as one's eyes become adjusted to the light filtering through the stained-glass windows, the scene is gradually discerned, the dim light bringing out the warm hues of the stone, and revealing the crossing, the south transept, and above all the chancel.

The nave is clearly subordinate to the chancel, being less in both length and height, and not so richly decorated. When first built, it was even shorter, consisting of only two bays; but a third bay was added later, and at the west end a narthex was built in 1906. The roof is of the wagon type and the floor is of marble. Along the aisles are the Stations of the Cross; these were carved by two Antwerp woodworkers, de Wint and Boeck. There is much stained glass by Burlison and Grylls, with a complicated iconography, well explained in the church guide; and a font with a soaring font-cover.

But impressive though the nave undoubtedly is, it is but the preparation for the chancel. Here is focussed the attentions of the worshippers as the drama of the Eucharist is played out and the sacrifice of Christ re-enacted. What a contrast to the churches of the eighteenth century, with their focus on pulpit and preaching! The chancel is lofty, with tierceron vault-ing. The great east window, with its complicated tracery, and the side windows, admit much more light than is granted to the nave. The rich carvings of the reredos (Fig.67) and the walls of the chancel, the sedilia, the marble flooring, the north and south chapels with their monuments all combine to make the chancel of Hoar Cross one of the culminating experiences of nineteenth-century architecture. Thorold says that 'it is a church to pray in'; it is more than that – above all, it is a church in which to receive the body and blood of the Lord Jesus.

Access: From Lichfield, take the A515 north. In Yoxall, take the first turning on the left past the church, and shortly after fork right and go through Hadley End to Hoar Cross, where the church is on the left.

The Collegiate Churches

DURING the twelfth and thirteenth centuries, a number of churches in England possessed an unusual status as 'royal free chapels' or 'royal peculiars' – that is, they were claimed by the king to be totally free from the ordinary jurisdiction of the bishop of the diocese in which they were geographically situated; and the king himself exercised the right of presentation (Denton). These claims were buttressed by papal grants of exemption from diocesan control. These churches were 'collegiate' – they consisted of a community of canons under the leadership of a dean. They therefore represented an important field of royal patronage, which was usually jealously safeguarded. Some of the collegiate churches arose from Anglo-Saxon minsters, and after the Norman Conquest, each canon in the college had his own separate prebend (i.e. a share in the revenues of the college).

The diocese of Coventry and Lichfield had an unusually large number of such churches within its territory: in Staffordshire, there were Gnosall, Penkridge, Stafford St Mary, Tettenhall and Wolverhampton St Peter; and there were others in Shropshire and Derbyshire. The case of Tamworth was somewhat different: the church here certainly became a royal college in the fourteenth century, but not a royal peculiar, because the diocesan bishop continued to exercise the right of patronage. These six collegiate churches are amongst the finest in the county, and the history of each is summarised below.

St Lawrence, Gnosall

If Staffordshire churches were better known, it is safe to say that Gnosall church (Fig.69), like Clifton Campville, would be famous throughout the country. For not only is it a magnificent building in its own right, displaying work of every medieval style, but its setting within the village is also outstanding. In the description which follows, I am much indebted to the excellent history of the church by John Roper which is available at St Lawrence's.

The derivation of the rather unusual name has not been determined precisely. The first reference to it is in Domesday Book, where it is referred to as Geneshale. There is no mention of any church or priest here, but this does not preclude such a presence. The scale and magnificence of the Norman building in the twelfth century, together with Gnosall's status as a collegiate

(Fig 69) **St Laurence, Gnosall**

(Fig 70) **St Laurence, Gnosall** *Norman chancel arch; Early English arcades.*

(Fig 71) **St Laurence, Gnosall** *Fine Norman columns in the south transept.*

(Fig 72) **St Laurence, Gnosall** *Norman triforium.*

distinguish from other collegiate churches belonging to the bishop. At the end of the next century, in 1292, Edward I tried to regain the patronage of Gnosall for the crown, but the attempt failed, and a jury found in favour of the bishop.

The greatest work at St Lawrence is the Norman crossing, now supporting the much later Perpendicular tower. The west arch of the crossing (Fig.70), facing the nave, displays a great variety of carving, including chevron or zigzag, billet, and the 'Greek key'. The south transept is also Norman and very fine, with blank arcading (Fig.71), internal stair turret and open triforium (Fig.72). In the next century, the thirteenth, the church was enlarged by the construction of aisles, separated from the nave by Early English arcades, with octagonal piers; lancet windows are still visible over the west door. In the fourteenth century, the east window of the chancel was inserted; this is of fine Decorated design, with flowing tracery typical of its age (Fig.38, p23). Finally in the fifteenth century, the Perpendicular age contributed the battlemented clerestory above the nave, the south chapel, and the tower. The latter is a splendid example of Perpendicular building, with eight pinnacles, and below them an ornamental frieze on all four sides. Just above the level of the roof of the nave, where the Perpendicular tower was built on to the supporting Norman crossing, project four corbels, one of which on the southwest corner depicts a hooded figure. Also carved in the walls of the tower is a chalice in the south wall and a shield below the frieze on each wall.

Access: From Stafford, take the A518 westwards towards Newport; after just over five miles, take the second turning on the right in the village for the church, which is then on the left.

St Michael and All Angels, Penkridge

The small town of Penkridge, close to the M6, is dominated by the fine tower of St Michael's, which can indeed be seen from the motorway (Fig.1, p7). The name of the town derives from the nearby Roman station of Pennocrucium, a name of Celtic origin meaning 'chief mound' (Greenslade and Stuart); this was situated on Watling Street (the modern A5), and

church, would imply that there was a predecessor Saxon building which is not now apparent.

In fact, Gnosall's status as a royal free chapel is somewhat anomalous. There is no direct evidence that there was a preceding Anglo-Saxon minster. By the twelfth century, however, Gnosall was certainly one of the group of royal peculiars, but during the reign of King Stephen (1135-54), the crown divested itself of the patronage of some of the group, and Gnosall, uniquely, was given to the diocesan bishop, the bishop of Coventry (Denton). It thus became difficult to

(Fig 73) **St Michael, Penkridge** *Early English arcades, Decorated east window, Perpendicular clerestory; roof not original.*

was a junction for other roads coming from the south and north-west. The town today is two miles north of the A5.

The origin of St Michael's is lost in the mists of antiquity: according to the church guide, the earliest record suggests that it was founded as a chantry chapel in 910-913 so that priests could say Mass for the souls of Saxon warriors killed in a battle with the Danes. The second account records that the church was founded as a collegiate church by King Edgar who had, in 970, made Penkridge his base to counter an invasion of Danes and Irish entering the country through Cheshire. After the Norman conquest, Penkridge was reconstituted as a royal chapel or 'peculiar' and the college of priests was re-established. In 1206, the deanery of Penkridge was given to the Archbishop of Dublin, and successive Archbishops were deans of Penkridge until the college was dissolved in 1547. In 1530, it is recorded that the staff of the college consisted of a Sub-dean, seven Pre-bendaries, two resident Canons, six Vicars, one High deacon, one Sub-deacon and one Sacrist. In addition to Penkridge, the college ministered to chapels at Dunston, Coppenhall, Stretton and Shareshill.

The present very fine church was begun around 1225, building first the chancel and then the nave. These are therefore Early English in style, with round

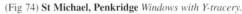

(Fig 74) **St Michael, Penkridge** *Windows with Y-tracery.*

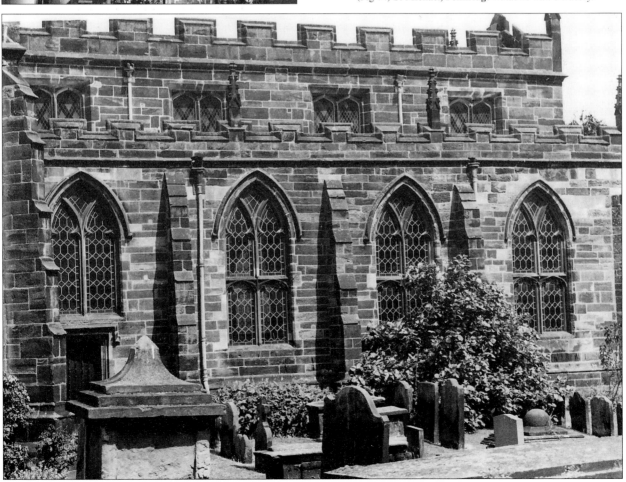

(Fig 75) **St Mary, Stafford**

piers and round capitals (Fig.73); there are lancet windows in the south wall of the chancel with Y-tracery which may or may not be original (Fig.74). In the fourteenth century (Decorated) was built the lower stages of the tower and south porch, and a large east window with flowing tracery was inserted in the chancel. In the Perpendicular age (fifteenth century), the upper stages of the tower were completed, with battlements, parapets and pinnacles; an upper storey was added to the porch; and the whole of the nave and chancel was given a clerestory, with battlements above. Thus St Michael's appears largely a Perpendicular church from outside, but an Early English one within.

In the chancel are some fifteenth-century choir-stalls which survive from the collegiate church, with misericords beneath. The screen dividing nave from chancel is made of wrought iron, and comes from South Africa, dated 1778. There is a wooden Perpendicular screen separating the chancel from the south chapel. Some outstanding monuments to the Littleton family, who lived at nearby Pillaton, are in the east end of the church. In the chancel are alabaster monuments to two Sir Edward Littletons, who died in 1558 and 1574 (Fig.114, p58) respectively. In the east end of the north chapel is a large standing two-tier monument to two further Sir Edward Littletons, who died in 1610 and 1629 (Fig.125, p61). The workmanship of all these is excellent.

Access: Penkridge is on the A449, between Stafford and Wolverhampton. The church is just to the west of the main road, in the centre of the town.

St Mary, Stafford

As befits the leading parish church in the county town, St Mary's is well situated in a spacious green sward (Fig.75), undisturbed by local traffic. At its west end, next to the south aisle, are the foundations of the Anglo-Saxon church of St Bertelin. He was an obscure eighth-century saint who lived on an island in the River Sow near Stafford; the church of St Bertoline at Barthomley in Cheshire is dedicated to him. His church in Stafford survived from the eleventh century to 1801, and in latter days was used as the local grammar school. His shrine is at Ilam, in north Staffordshire (p76).

St Mary's was one of the original five collegiate churches in Staffordshire, and was a Saxon foundation, serving as a minster church for a wide area before the development of the parish system in the eleventh century. None of the fabric of St Mary's, however, goes as far back as Saxon times, the oldest object in the church being the striking and unusual Norman font (Fig.94, p51), decorated with lions and said to show Byzantine influence related to a pilgrimage made by a twelfth-century bishop of Lichfield to the Holy Land.

St Mary's is a prominent landmark in Stafford by virtue of its octagonal tower which rises above the central crossing. The tower is Perpendicular, and was originally surmounted by a spire, which unfortunately fell into the chancel in 1594. The pinnacles on the tower date from Scott's restoration.

The nave is basically Early English (thirteen

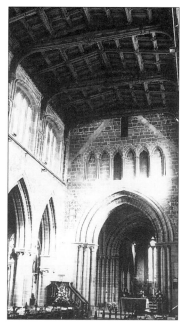

(Fig 76) **St Mary, Stafford** *The nave, with Early English north arcade, and Perpendicular clerestory and roof.*

(Fig 77) **St Editha, Tamworth** *The chancel.*

(Fig 78) **St Editha, Tamworth** *Tomb recesses in the north wall of the chancel.*

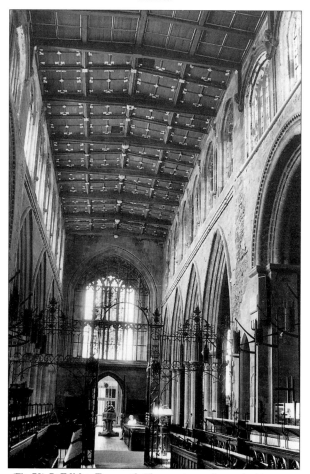

(Fig 79) **St Editha, Tamworth** *The crossing and nave, looking west. The nearest arch on the right is Norman, the further ones Decorated.*

century), though much restored by George Gilbert Scott in the 1840s. Above the arcades are a Perpendicular clerestory and low-pitched Perpendicular roof. The chancel is separated from the nave by the central crossing, and high up in the west wall of the crossing can be seen a series of blind arches and two windows indicating the level of the bell-ringers' chamber (Fig.76). At each end can be seen the marks of the earlier steeply-pitched thirteenth-century roof. The windows of the north and south aisles show Perpendicular and Decorated tracery respectively. In the north aisle is a monument to Izaak Walton, author of *The Compleat Angler*, who was baptised in the church in 1593. The chancel is a little later than the nave, the piers supporting the arcades being slenderer and dating from the Decorated period (*c.*1300). It is darker, having lost its clerestory in the Victorian reconstruction.

The north transept is perhaps the most interesting part of the building. Inside is the tomb of Sir Edward Aston (died 1568) and his wife – two recumbent effigies on a tomb-chest, the sides being decorated with figurines and twisted colonettes. The effigy of Sir Edward unfortunately lost his head when a jury box was being erected above the tomb when the church was used as an Assize Court in the eighteenth century. Beyond the tomb, on the north wall on each side of the door there is blank arcading in the Decorated manner, with steep gabling. Above is a Perpendicular clerestory. Go outside here to admire the beautiful north doorway, with leaf capitals and above fleurons and ball-flowers in the arch.

Access: In the town centre.

St Editha, Tamworth

St Editha's is an under-rated church: many would claim that it is the finest town church in Staffordshire, and I would be inclined to agree.

No site in Staffordshire, possibly apart from Lichfield, has a more venerable history than this medium-sized town situated pleasantly on the river Tame. Offa, King of Mercia from 757 to 796, built a palace here, and the earliest reference to Tamworth is from a document dated 781. In the eighth century, both Repton in Derbyshire and Tamworth appear to have

(Fig 80) **St Editha, Tamworth**
Perpendicular tower.

bishop retained the right of institution to the deanery and the prebends; Denton). It is dedicated to St Editha (see p95), daughter of King Edward of Wessex, granddaughter of Alfred the Great, sister of King Athelstan and niece of Aethelflaed. She was married at Tamworth to the Danish king Sihtric in 926, and Tamworth is the only town in Staffordshire to retain some Danish street-names. Athelstan gave his sister the royal residence at Tamworth where as a widow she established a convent. She died in 946.

Tamworth is dominated by the twin landmarks of the Norman castle and the parish church (Fig. 5, p10). The church is a large, impressive building, with a west Perpendicular tower (Fig.80), Decorated nave (Figs. 79, 81), and chancel (Fig. 77) and a Perpendicular clerestory which runs the whole length of the church, giving it an architectural unity which is, in fact, rather spurious. For closer inspection inside reveals two large, typical Norman arcades at the north and south sides (Fig. 81), between the nave and chancel, there being no chancel arch. Originally the church was cruciform, with a central tower. This was destroyed in a disastrous fire in 1345, causing both nave and chancel to be rebuilt in the Decorated manner, the east and west arches of the crossing being removed.

The chancel is spacious and dignified; three recesses in the north wall (Fig.78), separating the chancel from the north chapel, are occupied by effigies. The first two (from the west) are much deformed, but the third is an alabaster monument to Sir John Ferrers and his wife (1512). Between the nave and chancel is an eighteenth-century wrought-iron screen reminiscent of that in All Saints, Derby (the cathedral), but of much simpler design. The roofs of

functioned as capitals of Mercia, but by the ninth century Mercia was in decline and both towns were sacked by the invading Danes in 874. Tamworth was later recaptured by Edward the Elder, son of Alfred the Great; his sister Aethelflaed (the Lady of the Mercians) fortified it in 913 and died there five years later. The town was again captured by the Danes in 943, but by 963 it was again in Saxon hands and a church was founded by King Edgar, possibly with collegiate status.

So the church originated in Saxon times, but documentary evidence of Tamworth's status as a royal free chapel is rather scanty: a college of five canons was apparently re-founded during the reign of William the Conqueror, and lasted until 1547. It became a royal college but not a royal peculiar (i.e. the diocesan

(Fig 81) **St Editha, Tamworth** *The roof, clerestory and nave looking east.*

(Fig 82) **St Michael, Tettenhall**

the nave and aisles are fine, and decorated with bosses (that of the south aisle being the best). Below part of the south aisle is a crypt. The tower is remarkable for the double spiral staircase in the south-west turret. In the north wall of the tower is the finest monument in the church to Sir John Ferrers (1680); this was commissioned from Grinling Gibbons, but is thought in fact to have been carved by Arnold Quellin, with cherubs by C.G.Cibber.

Access: Tamworth is two miles north of Watling Street (A5), northeast of Birmingham. St Editha's church is at the highest point of the town centre, north of the castle.

St Michael and All Angels, Tettenhall

Tettenhall, now a pleasant suburb of Wolverhampton, has an impressive ecclesiastical history: for this unlikely place was also one of the original collegiate churches of the diocese of Coventry and Lichfield. It was the site of a battle in 910 between Anglo-Saxons and Danes, and following the Anglo-Saxon victory a Saxon church was established there. This has disappeared without trace. By the time of the Domesday survey (1086) there was a deanery and a college of secular canons, the dean being appointed by the Crown and not by the diocesan bishop. This lasted until the Reformation, when the college was dissolved and its property was sold to a local gentleman, Walter

Wrottesley, who also acquired the advowson; but it remained a royal free chapel. According to the 'Little Guide' of Staffordshire (Masefield), the medieval church consisted of two surviving Norman piers and capitals, Early English arcades, a Decorated north aisle

(Fig 83) **St Michael, Tettenhall** *The interior.*

and a Perpendicular clerestory, with a fine fifteenth-century parclose screen around the Wrottesley chapel.

Disaster struck St Michael's on 2 February 1950, when the building apart from the tower was totally destroyed by fire. So the opportunity was provided for the design of a modern church, the major constraint being the survival of the Perpendicular west tower. It would have been understandable, though pusillanimous, if the new building had been in the style of Victorian Gothic, of the sort that might have

(Fig 84) **St Peter, Wolverhampton**

been built in the 1880s. On the other hand, a totally modern design might have married ill with the medieval tower. In the event, the new church avoids both these pitfalls: although traditionally arranged with nave and aisles, it is not in any recognisable medieval style; and it certainly cannot be portrayed as an example of avant-garde architecture.

The church stands on rising ground commanding views across Wolverhampton, and approaching from the south the most arresting feature is the triple-gabled façade of the south aisle (Fig.82), a little reminiscent of the work of Street at Brewood (Fig.261, p115). The interior (Fig.83) is light, and at first glance appears medieval, but the piers are unusually short, and are surmounted by carved capitals of unusual leaf design. The oak timbers of the roof and the copper lights of the nave combine to give a warm atmosphere. In the chancel are four guardian angels, and a remarkable east window, with modern tracery filled with stained glass representing Christ in Glory above, and the Last Supper below.

Access: From Wolverhampton centre proceed along the A41 towards Newport for two miles; St Michael's is on an elevation on the right, shortly after the A41 crosses the Staffordshire and Worcestershire canal.

St Peter, Wolverhampton

The history of Wolverhampton appears to start in 985 when a lady called Wulfrun became possessed of the

manor of Hantun (or high town); nine years later, she endowed the minster church there with extensive lands, and by the end of the eleventh century the settlement was known as Wolvrenehamptonia. From the first, the church had collegiate status, and it was also a Royal Free chapel, responsible only to the king and the pope. In 1479, the deaneries of Wolverhampton and Windsor were united and alone of the royal free chapels of Staffordshire, Wolverhampton's status as a royal peculiar survived the Reformation. It was not until 1848 that the deanery was suppressed and for the first time St Peter's came under the authority of the Bishops of Lichfield.

The church we see today standing proudly in the town centre (Fig.84) is built of red sandstone and gives an overwhelming impression of a prosperous Perpendicular edifice – yet in fact there are four distinct building periods. Earliest is the base of the crossing, and the south transept; these date from the late thirteenth or early fourteenth century – note the Decorated east window of the south transept. The nave, aisles and clerestory are mid-fifteenth century, with Perpendicular windows throughout. The central tower of four storeys, replete with battlements and pinnacles and the north transept are late Perpendicular, and date from the early sixteenth century. Finally, the chancel (Fig.85) and west front are a Victorian rebuilding, dating from 1865.

The interior is equally impressive. The nave (Fig.86) is of five bays, one remarkable feature being the medieval stone pulpit (Fig.87) which winds round

(Fig 85) **St Peter,
Wolverhampton**
The chancel.

(Fig 86) **St Peter, Wolverhampton** *Perpendicular arcades.*

(Fig 87) **St Peter,
Wolverhampton**
*Perpendicular
stone pulpit.*

one of the southern pillars, the entrance to the pulpit being guarded rather enigmatically by a lion. Above the arcades are rows of double clerestory windows which reflect the wealth of the wool and other merchants of the fifteenth century, undisturbed by the Wars of the Roses. The roof is of low pitch, and is embossed, the bosses having been recently recoloured.

The north transept, now the War Memorial chapel, contains the tomb of Thomas Lane and his wife Catherine (1585) made by Royleys of Burton upon Trent (Fig.115, p59). The recumbent effigies lie side by side, and around the tomb-chest are statuettes of their seven daughters and five sons. Next to the Lane tomb is the monument to Col. John Lane who helped Charles II to escape after the Battle of Worcester in 1651; in the carving below is an oak tree bearing the crown, symbolising the hiding of the king in the oak at Boscobel.

The south transept, now the Lady Chapel, is separated from the crossing by an attractive fifteenth-century parclose screen (Fig. 140, p65). Glass in the east window portrays the descent of Christ from Jesse, the father of David. Also in this transept is another Royley tomb, that of John Leveson (1575). But the most striking monument in St Peter's is the standing bronze effigy of Admiral Sir Richard Leveson, made by Hubert Le Sueur in 1634. After the destruction of the base of the statue by Commonwealth soldiers, it was taken to Lilleshall for protection, and restored to St Peter's after the Restoration. Le Sueur was Charles I's favourite sculptor, responsible for the monument to the Duke of Buckingham in Westminster Abbey and for the equestrian statue of the king himself at Charing Cross.

Access: St Peter's *is* the centre of Wolverhampton.

Works of Art in Staffordshire Churches

Norman fonts

There is a great variety of fonts in Staffordshire, and of the fifty-eight pre-Reformation fonts, a handful of Norman examples are by far the most impressive. Geometric patterns, and animal and human representations, often bizarre, are shown with great skill and inventiveness. The finest are Armitage, Bradley, Checkley, Ilam, Longdon, Pipe Ridware (now at Hamstall Ridware), Stafford St Mary and Wolverhampton (St Mary Bushbury). Of the later medieval fonts, Kinver (Fig.269, p119) and Alrewas are excellent.

The font with the best Norman geometric patterning is at Bradley, with bands of ornament running horizontally around the bowl (Fig.88). From above downwards there are cable, billet, fret and key patterns, and prominently below the key

(Fig 88) **St Mary and All Saints, Bradley** *Norman font with geometric patterning.*

pattern is a sunken star ornament twice the height of the others. Jeavons (1949-50) points out the close resemblance between the font at Bradley with the badly damaged and poorly displayed font at Church Eaton, (Fig.89) three miles to the west. This was dug up in the churchyard, and during restoration has been inverted so that the original bottom rim is now in the centre of the bowl. Bearing this in mind, the ornamentation can be seen to resemble Bradley very closely. He also found close similarities with the font at Edgmond, fifteen miles to the west in Shropshire, and postulated the existence of a local school of masons in Lilleshall Abbey, a few miles to the south of Edgmond. The font previously at Pipe Ridware now resides at Hamstall Ridware and is another masterpiece of Norman geometrical design (Fig.90). Below the rim are two plain bands of ornament intertwining around the whole bowl, and

(Fig 89) **St Editha, Church Eaton** *The damaged Norman font.*

(Fig 90) **St Michael, Hamstall Ridware** *Norman font originally at Pipe Ridware.*

below are intersecting circles of pellet ornament.

At Longdon (Fig. 91) there is the lovely and unusual combination of a Norman bowl standing on an Early English stem. The bowl has an upper band of stylised interlocking leaves, and below a much deeper zone of a diagonally carved fluted design. The stem is from a capital in the nave of Lichfield Cathedral showing stiff-leaf carving.

Two fonts show animal designs on the bowl – Checkley has a well-bred donkey flanked by symbolic palm-trees, with formal diagonal patterning around the rest of the font (Fig.92). In contrast, Ilam has a chaotic jumble of crudely executed figures, both animal and human, assembled under a series of arcades (Fig.93, a,

(Fig 91) **St James, Longdon** *Norman bowl standing on an Early English stem.*

49

b and c). On one panel are two human figures, the one on the left holding up the right hand in blessing, the other figure appearing to be a woman. To the left of this panel is a monster with a serpent-like head and neck turned backwards, with what appears to be a human head held in its open jaws. The panel to the right of the human figures shows the Agnus Dei (Jeavons). The interpretation of the other panels is quite obscure.

The unusual font at St Mary's, Stafford, is difficult to classify; it certainly shows foreign influence, possibly Byzantine or Italian, and is quatrefoil in cross-section, with lions crouching at the base (Fig.94).

Strangest of all, perhaps, is the font at Armitage (Fig.95). Now installed in a comfortably Victorian neo-Norman church, this shows grotesque paired human figures under a series of arcades. The figures are malproportioned, with large heads and prominent eyes, and again interpretation of the carving is beyond us. But there is no doubting the quality of the workmanship of this early Norman font.

The Swynnerton Statue

At St Mary's, Swynnerton is a magnificent thirteenth-century seated sandstone statue of Christ 'in Majesty (Fig.96a, b); this was

(Fig 92) **St Mary, Checkley** *Norman font: a donkey flanked by palm-trees?*

(Fig 93a,b,c) **Holy Cross, Ilam** *Three faces of the Norman font, showing human and animal figures.*

(Fig 95) **St John, Armitage** *Norman font with grotesque human figures under a series of arches.*

(Fig 96a, b) **St Mary, Swynnerton** *Thirteenth-century Christ in Majesty, seven feet tall.*

(Fig 94) **St Mary, Stafford** *Unusual Norman font, said to show Byzantime influence.*

may have been taken down from the cathedral at the time of the civil disturbances and transported twenty-four miles to Swynnerton; but this suggestion has not found favour with all (Cocke).

The seven-feet-tall statue is in the south chapel of St Mary's church, Swynnerton. Our Lord is portrayed with great dignity, displaying the wound of the spear in the side of the chest, and the mark of the nail in the left hand. The right upper limb has been lost and there has been damage to the face, but in spite of this the figure is very moving. The chapel is currently used as a vestry, which really means that the statue is not displayed to full advantage. The suggestion has been made that it should be housed at Lichfield Cathedral where it could be suitably exhibited, and appreciated by thousands of people who would never see it at Swynnerton. In general, I think it is a shame for parish churches to lose their treasures: but here in a vestry is the finest treasure in any Staffordshire church, and I think it deserves something better, preferably still in St Mary's.

Monumental Effigies 1270-1700

In the following pages are illustrations of thirty-eight monuments from Staffordshire churches. I have grouped these together, in preference to including them under the entries of their respective churches, in order that the reader may see the

apparently found some time before 1813 under the floor of the south chapel when a vault was being repaired (Cobb). Its provenance is completely unknown, but it is clear that here is a little-known work of art of outstanding quality. It is so good that the Victoria and Albert museum originally wished to exhibit it in the 'Age of Chivalry' exhibition in 1987-88.

From the style of the drapery, (known as the 'broad-fold style', which originated in Rheims and elsewhere *c.*1220-1240; Pevsner), it is likely that the work is from the mid-late thirteenth century, but when, how or why it was moved to Swynnerton is quite unknown. The most plausible suggestion is that it came from the gable at the west end of Lichfield Cathedral. Thomas Fuller's Church History (1655) contains an etching of the west front of the cathedral drawn before the Civil War showing a seated statue (presumably of Christ) in the central gable; 'its place was later occupied by a statue of Charles II and, since 1869, by a new statue of the Saviour' (Cobb). It is conjectured that the statue

gradual evolution in style over a period of over four hundred years. In nearly every case, however, further information about each subject may be found by reference to the entry of the church concerned. The illustrations are summarised in the accompanying Table (p53).

Monumental effigies abound in Staffordshire churches – Jeavons (f,g,h) listed nearly 200 between 1270 and 1700, and there are of course many more from the eighteenth and nineteenth centuries. Two wooden effigies at Weston-under-Lizard (Fig.98) survive in good condition; these are of unknown knights, and date from the early fourteenth century. Apart from these, the early effigies were of stone, the oldest being probably that of a priest at Enville, dated about 1270 (Fig.97). From then until the end of the fourteenth century, a succession of stone effigies may be found. Fig.99 shows a stone effigy at Draycott-in-the-Moors of an unknown knight, shown sheathing or unsheathing his sword, and with his legs crossed; this

(Fig 97) **St Mary, Enville** *Stone effigy of a priest, c.1270.*

dates from *c.*1300. The stone effigy of the knight at Norbury (Fig.101; see also Fig.223, p98.) is from the first half of the fourteenth century.

(Fig 98a, b) **St Andrew, Weston-under-Lizard** *Two wooden effigies of knights, 1300-1320.*

(Fig 99) **St Margaret, Draycott-in-the-Moors** *Stone effigy of an unknown knight, c.1300.*

(Fig 100) **St Werburgh, Hanbury** *Supposed effigy of Sir John de Hanbury – but see text.*

Fig.104 shows one of the two stone effigies of ladies found at Statfold, dating from *c.*1390. Again the subject is unknown, and the lady is shown with her hands clasped in prayer and holding her heart in her hands. By 1400 alabaster had come into general use, and between 1400 and 1600 there is only one further stone effigy, that of John Stanley at Elford (Fig.105), the boy who died in 1460 after being struck by a tennis-ball.

The earliest use of alabaster is in the west doorway of the Priory of St Mary, Tutbury (Fig.18, p15), *c.*1160-1170. Until recently it was believed that the earliest alabaster effigy in England was at Hanbury (Fig.100), dating from 1303. Recent work suggests that this effigy is later (*c.*1340; see p104). Alabaster is a compact marble-like form of gypsum (calcium sulphate), and was quarried at Chellaston, a few miles south of Derby, and at Tutbury in Staffordshire.

Gardner points out that alabaster is soft, easy to work, and is well-suited for taking colour and gilding. Because of these properties, alabaster was favoured for memorial effigies for over three hundred years.

Table of Illustrated Effigies *(Figs. 97-133 incl.)*

Church	Subject	Date (c.)	Material
Enville	priest	1270	stone
Weston-under-Lizard	two knights	1300-20	wood
Draycott-in-the-Moors	knight	1300	stone
Hanbury	knight	1340	alabaster
Norbury	le Botiller	1310-42	stone
Elford	knight	1370	alabaster
Audley	knight	1385	alabaster
Statfold	lady	1390	stone
Elford	John Stanley	1460	stone
Madeley	Egerton	1522	alabaster
Elford	Smythe	1525	"
Patshull	Astley	1532	"
Stowe-by-Chartley	Devereux	1537	"
Clifton Campville	Vernon	1545	"
Draycott-in-the-Moors	Draycott	1559	"
Enville	Grey	1559	"
Brewood	Thomas Giffard	1560	"
Penkridge	Littleton	1574	"
Wolverhampton	Lane	1575	"
Seighford	Bowyer	1593	"
Hanbury	Adderley	1595	"
Blithfield	Bagot	1596	"
Sandon	Erdeswick	1601	"
Ashley	Gerard	1602	
Draycott-in-the-Moors	Draycott	1602	"
Eccleshall	Overton	1609	"
Brewood	John Giffard	1613	"
Hanbury	Charles Egerton	1624	"
Penkridge	Littleton	1610-29	"
Forton	Skrymsher	1633	"
Blore	Bassett	1601-40	"
Rolleston	Mosley	1638	"
Ilam	Lady Cromwell	1650	"
Hanbury	Puritan ladies	1629, 1657	"
Hanbury	Egerton	1662	"
Brewood	Moreton	1630, 1669	"
Patshull	Astley	1687	"

After the early figure at Hanbury, there are no further alabaster effigies until the last thirty years of the fourteenth century, from which period examples may be seen at Elford (*c.*1370; Fig.102), and Audley (*c.*1385; Fig.103); the knights are shown clad in armour of the period. In the fifteenth century, the only effigies are rather worn ones at Gnosall and Kinver. But at the beginning of the sixteenth century, there is a remarkable resurgence of alabaster effigies all over the county and spreading into neighbouring shires.

The industry was first centred in Nottingham, whence alabaster was sent all over the country and also to the continent in the late fourteenth and fifteenth centuries. In the later fifteenth century, however,

(Fig 101) **St Peter, Norbury** *Effigy of Ralph le Botiller (1310 or 1342?)*

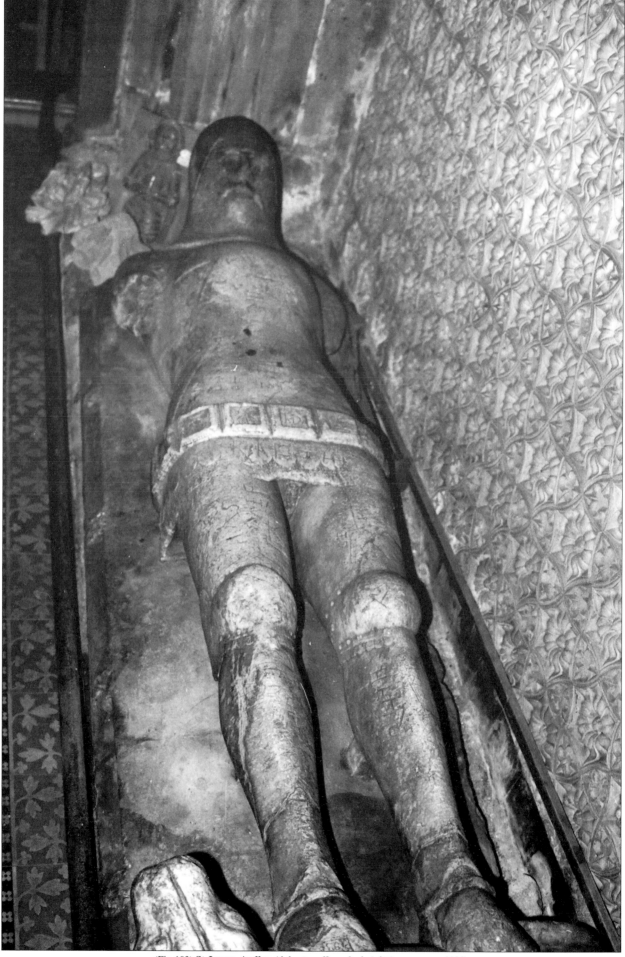

(Fig 103) **St James, Audley** *Alabaster effigy of a knight in armour, c.1385.*

(Fig 102) **St Peter, Elford** *Alabaster effigy of a knight in armour, c.1370.*

(Fig 107) **St Peter, Elford** *Effigy of Sir William Smythe (died 1525) and his wives, Lady Isabella Neville and Anne Staunton.*

Nottingham's supremacy was increasingly challenged by workers at Burton upon Trent. From then onwards, Nottingham concentrated on religious statuary and Burton became the dominant centre for monumental effigies and slabs. Early work from Burton may be seen at Tamworth, Uttoxeter and Leigh. The pace then accelerates, with memorials commissioned for Elford, Patshull, Stowe-by-Chartley, Clifton Campville, Madeley (Figs.106 to 110) and at other places outside the county.

Throughout the medieval period, and indeed until the end of the sixteenth century, the effigies were portrayed recumbent on the tomb-chest, usually in an attitude of conventional devotion, with the hands clasped in prayer. Details of armour, vestments and garments may be of considerable help in dating the monuments, for the inscriptions cannot always be trusted, and monuments were sometimes erected some years either before or after the death of the person concerned. Around the tomb-chest, it was customary to carve small figures known as figurines or 'weepers'. These might represent the offspring of the deceased; in other tombs, saints or angels might be portrayed, sometimes with heraldic shields or regalia.

(Fig 104) **All Saints, Statfold** *Fourteenth-century stone effigy of a lady.*

(Fig 105) **St Peter, Elford** *Stone effigy of the young John Stanley, struck by a tennis-ball, c.1460.*

Two of the first Burton sculptors whose names are known were Henry Harpur and William Moorecock, who were probably responsible for the tombs at Cubley and Ashover in Derbyshire; in Staffordshire they were probably responsible for the tomb and incised alabaster cover

for Randolph Egerton and his wife at Madeley (Fig.106). A little later was Richard Parker, who made the altar tomb of the first Earl of Rutland at Bottesford amongst others. He died in 1571, and during the working life of Parker and his predecessors the output of the Burton alabasterers achieved a very high standard.

It is, however, the workshop of Richard and Gilbert Royley, father and son, which came to dominate the output of Burton upon Trent. Their earliest identifiable work is a slab at Pitchford in Shropshire (1534), and their latest at Peatling Magna, Leicestershire (1597). The early examples from the Royley workshop were quite good, but from about 1550 they achieved a dominance which was to last for thirty years. They became extremely conservative, harking back to the medieval past and ignoring the new ideas stemming from the Renaissance.

Some commentators have been very scathing about their productions; thus Esdaile (1946): 'How in so brief a space as thirty years monumental effigies could have degenerated as they did at Burton is astonishing. Parker's work is very fine; that of the Royleys … .is frankly very bad indeed.' F.A.Greenhill (1976) concurs: 'The Renaissance seems to have passed them by, and their later work is hidebound to a degree.'

The accompanying illustrations afford an opportunity for comparison of the earlier work at Burton from Elford (1525; Fig. 107), Patshull (1532; Fig.108), Stowe-by-Chartley (1537; Fig.109) and Clifton Campville (1545; Fig.110) with the later effigies from Draycott-in-the-Moors (1559; Fig.111), Enville (1559; Fig.112), Brewood (1560; Fig.113), Penkridge (1574; Fig.114), Wolverhampton St Peter (1575; Fig.115), Seighford (1593; Fig.116), Hanbury (1595; Fig.117) and Blithfield (1596; Fig.118); all this group probably emanated from the Royleys' workshop.

Then in the 1580s a Dutchman, Jasper Hollemans, settled in Burton and a breath of fresh air and creativity swept away outmoded design. Renaissance themes were now in full swing, and the Staffordshire memorials of the early seventeenth century show a

(Fig 106) **All Saints, Madeley** *Figurines around the tomb-chest of Randolph and Isabella Egerton (1522).*

(Fig 108) **St Mary, Patshull** *Effigies of Sir John Astley and his wife (1532).*

(Fig 109) **St John, Stowe-by-Chartley** *Effigy of Sir Walter Devereux (died 1537) and his wives.*

(Fig 111) **St Margaret, Draycott-in-the-Moors** *Sir Philip Draycott (1559).*

clear break with the productions of the Royleys. Jeavons (h) claims that the memorials at Sandon (1601; Fig.119), Eccleshall (1609; Fig.122), Ashley (1602-17; Fig.120), Penkridge (1610-29; Fig.125), and Blore (sometime between 1601 and 1643; Fig.127) are from Hollemans' workshop. These are monuments on a substantial scale and breathe an air of Renaissance self-confidence contrasting with the ostentatious piety of earlier days. Indeed, by the time we arrive at the very grand late Stuart memorial to Sir Richard Astley and his wives at Patshull (1687; Fig.133) we are clearly on the verge of the eighteenth century.

Throughout the seventeenth century, it became very characteristic to portray subjects kneeling in prayer rather than recumbent. The earliest examples in Staffordshire are the wives of Samson Erdeswick at Sandon (1601; Fig.119) and Bishop Overton at Eccleshall (1609; Fig.122), where the ladies are shown kneeling above the effigies of their respective husbands. Later examples are shown at Ilam (Fig.129) and Brewood (Fig.132). The remarkable busts of the Puritan ladies at Hanbury (Fig.130) are unique and

(Fig 110) **St Andrew, Clifton Campville** *Effigies of Sir John Vernon, (died 1545) and his wife.*

(Fig 112) **St Mary, Enville** *Effigies of Thomas Grey and his wife (1559) with children around the tomb-chest.*

(Fig 113a, b) **St Mary and St Chad, Brewood** *Effigies of Sir Thomas Giffard (died 1560) and his wives, with figurines around the tomb-chest.*

(Fig 116a, b) **St Chad, Seighford** *Tomb-chest of William Bowyer (died 1593) and his wife, with figurines on the sides.*

(Fig 114) **St Michael, Penkridge** *Tomb-chest of Sir Edward Littleton (died 1574) and his wife.*

(Fig 115) **St Peter, Wolverhampton** *Tomb-chest of Thomas Lane and his wife (1585).*

(Fig 117) **St Werburgh, Hanbury** *Figurines around the tomb-chest of Ralph Adderley (died 1595).*

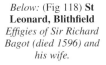

Below: (Fig 118) **St Leonard, Blithfield** *Effigies of Sir Richard Bagot (died 1596) and his wife.*

(Fig 119) **All Saints, Sandon** *Effigy of Samson Erdeswick, the antiquary, with his wives kneeling above. Made in 1601, probably by Hollemans.*

(Fig 120) **St John the Baptist, Ashley** *Large alabaster monument to Sir Gilbert Gerard (died 1593) and Lady Anne Gerard (died 1602).*

very entertaining in their attitude of prim disapproval. More conventional effigies continued to be produced, e.g. at Draycott-in-the-Moors (1602; Fig.121), Brewood (1613; Fig.123), Forton (1633; Fig.126), Hanbury (1624, 1662; Figs.124, 131) and Rolleston (1638; Fig.128), but Burton's days as a workshop of importance were drawing to a close, and from about the middle of the seventeenth century the centre of production moved to London.

Monuments from the eighteenth and nineteenth

(Fig 121) **St Margaret, Draycott-in-the-Moors** *John and Elizabeth Draycott (1607).*

(Fig 122) **Holy Trinity, Eccleshall** *Monument of Bishop Overton (died 1609) and his wives, probably by Hollemans.*

(Fig 123 and b) *below and bottom:* **St Mary and St Chad, Brewood** *A more traditional effigy of John Giffard (died 1613) and his wife, with figurines around the tomb-chest.*

centuries at Ilam, Okeover and Weston-under-Lizard are shown accompanying the descriptions of the respective churches.

Medieval stained glass

Glass was manufactured in Staffordshire during the Middle Ages, the main centres of production being around Abbot's Bromley and Rugeley (Marks). In the late fifteenth century, Robert Power, a glazier from Burton upon Trent became well known, his finest work probably being in the collegiate church of Tattershall in Lincolnshire; in Staffordshire, his work has been identified at Hamstall Ridware, Blore, and Broughton (q.v.).

Although about forty Staffordshire churches contain some medieval stained glass (Jeavons, 1949-50), the quality is not usually very high, and the extent is often small. There are, however, some exceptions. The finest

(Fig 124) **St Werburgh, Hanbury** *Semi-reclining effigy of Charles Egerton (died 1624).*

(Fig 125) **St Michael, Penkridge** *Part of the two-tiered monument to Sir Edward Littleton (died 1610) and his wife, and to Sir Edward Littleton (died 1629) and his wife.*

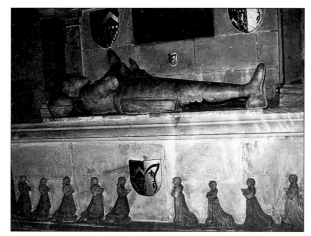

(Fig 126) **All Saints, Forton** *Effigies and tomb-chest of Sir Thomas Skrymsher (died 1633) and his wife.*

(Fig 131) **St Werburgh, Hanbury** *Recumbent effigy of Sir John Egerton (died 1662).*

(Fig 128) **St Mary, Rolleston** *Effigy of Sir Edward Mosley (1638).*

(Fig 132) **St Mary and St Chad, Brewood** *The Moreton monument – to Edward Moreton (died 1630) and to Matthew Moreton (died 1669) and their wives.*

(Fig 129) **Holy Cross, Ilam** *Kneeling monument to Lady Cromwell and her children (mid-17th century).*

Below: (Fig 133) **St Mary, Patshull** *The very grand late Stuart memorial to Sir Richard Astley (died 1687) and his wives.*

(Fig 130) **St Werburgh, Hanbury** *The Puritan ladies: Mrs Agard (died 1628) and her daughter Mrs Woollocke (died 1657).*

(Fig 127) **St Bartholomew, Blore** *Part of the huge Bassett monument, made at some date between 1601 and 1640.*

example is the exquisite fifteenth-century figure of the Virgin Mary at Hamstall Ridware (Fig. 134). Figs.135-137 show good glass from Hanbury, Whittington near Lichfield, and Seighford respectively. The churches at Checkley, Enville, Leigh, Okeover and Trysull also contain some good examples. There is, of course, a vast amount of Victorian glass, some of which is very good (e.g. at Cheddleton, Madeley and Tutbury), but much is undistinguished; consideration of this is beyond the scope of this work.

Woodwork
Medieval Screens

The oldest screen in Staffordshire is at Clifton Campville, separating the south aisle from the chapel beyond (Fig. 138a). The wainscot has two tiers of quatrefoil squints, and above are a series of

(Fib 136) **St Giles, Whittington** *A kneeling donor.*

(Fig 134) **St Michael, Hamstall Ridware** *The Virgin Mary from a Crucifixion scene.*

(Fig 137) **St Chad, Seighford** *Head of female saint.*

colonettes or shafts, with bases, annulets, and capitals supporting delicate trefoil tracery of the Decorated period (early fourteenth century). The other screens at this church are later: the rood dividing the nave from the chancel is Perpendicular (Fig. 138b). There is a central doorway, and on each side the screen is divided into six bays by vertical mullions which run up to the top beam below which is plate tracery; the wainscot has two bands of quatrefoils in circles, and below this run a series of cusped semicircular arches. Later still is

(Fig 135) **St Werburgh, Hanbury** *The Crucifixion with the robe of the Father.*

(Fig 138a) **St Andrew, Clifton Campville** *Three screeens (a) Early fourteenth century;*

(Fig 138) **St Andrew, Clifton Campville** (b) *above: late fifteenth century; (c) right: dated 1634.*

(Fig 140) **St Peter, Wolverhampton** *Perpendicular screen, south transept.*

(Fig 139a, b) **All Saints, King's Bromley** *Perpendicular screen, possibly the finest in Staffordshire.*

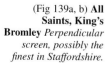

the screen dividing the chancel from the south chapel (Fig. 138c). This is dated 1634. At the top of the wainscot, and again along the top beam of the screen are bands of Renaissance strapwork, and further strapwork is seen vertically in the central mullion which divides the wainscot into two. Above the wainscot are seventeen shafts with trefoiled heads merging into an intersecting arcade.

The Perpendicular screen at King's Bromley, though somewhat restored, is possibly the finest in Staffordshire (Fig. 139a). The tracery is most intricate, and all is original except that in the two outer bays on each side. Branches sprout from each mullion, and entwine round each other, bearing leaves, flowers and fruit, and also two

(Fig 141) **St Bartholomew, Blore** *Perpendicular screen.*

monks' heads with open mouths (Fig.139b). Above the central doorway are vertical bands of tracery laterally, and between them a horizontal band above and below which are rows of quatrefoils.

The screen enclosing the south transept at Wolverhampton St Peter is beautifully and intricately carved (Fig.140), with upward coving a little reminiscent of the fine screen at Mobberley, Cheshire. Another slightly less ornate Perpendicular screen divides the north chapel from the aisle at Blore (Fig.141). In the lower half, the wainscot is solid, with a horizontal band of a chain motif, and cusped tracery below. The pattern is repeated above the openwork, with complex carving along the top beam and open tracery of great variety separating the vertical mullions. Rather similar Perpendicular screens may be seen at Madeley and Trysull (Figs.142, 143).

Seventeenth-century pulpits

The series of seventeenth-century pulpits of high quality begins with that at Wednesbury, dated 1611.

(Fig 142) **All Saints, Madeley** *The Perpendicular screen.*

(Fig 143) **All Saints, Trysull** *Perpendicular screen.*

(Fig 145) **St Margaret, Betley** *Jacobean pulpit.*

(Fig 146) **St John the Baptist, Mayfield** *Jacobean pulpit.*

The most elaborate pulpit in the county is that at Alstonefield (1637; Fig.144). This is a two decker, carved still in Elizabethan style, with texts inscribed on the back. Of a similar period are the pulpits at Betley, Mayfield and Trysull (Figs.145-147) the latter accompanied by a chest similarly carved. A little later is the pulpit at Sandon (*c.*1644; Fig.148), with blank arches as at Betley, but here surmounted by an exceptionally fine tester or sounding-board. Finest of all, perhaps, is that at Whittington, near Lichfield (Fig.149). This is dated 1671, and is supposed originally to come from Lichfield Cathedral. The style has now progressed into the classical, and the pulpit stands on an elegant twisted baluster stem. Another fine pulpit with tester is at Weston-under-Lizard (1701; Fig.150).

Altar-rails, choir-stalls, bench-ends and box-pews
The altar-rails at Blore (Fig.151) and Farewell (Fig.152) date from the mid-seventeenth century, and

show twisted balusters. Much more ornate, and probably a little later in date, is the remarkable and very rare communion rail at Mayfield (Fig.153), which shows a profusion of carved flowers and leaves, pierced panels and twisted balusters. The bench-ends

(Fig 144) **St Peter, Alstonefield** *Two-decker pulpit (1637).*

Above: (Fig 147) **All Saints, Trysull**
Jacobean pulpit.

Right: (Fig 149) **St Giles, Whittington**
*Pulpit and sounding-board in classical
style (1671), originally in Lichfield
cathedral.*

Far right: (Fig 150) **St Andrew,
Weston-under-Lizard** *Pulpit with
sounding-board, c.1701.*

(Fig 148) **All Saints, Sandon** *Pulpit with sounding-board (c.1644).*

(Fig 151) **St Bartholomew, Blore** *Choir-stalls and altar rail.*

(Fig 152) **St Bartholomew, Farewell** *Altar rail.*

(Fig 153) **St John the Baptist, Mayfield** *Communion rail.*

at Mayfield are also excellent, as are the box-pews at Alstonefield (Fig.154), Broughton and Stone. The rather primitive choir-stalls at Blore show poppyhead decoration (Fig.155), and beneath some sixteenth-century stalls at Farewell are a few misericords. At Walsall, there is an extensive set of misericords (Fig.156) and some good bench-ends (Fig.157). Even more impressive misericords may be seen at Enville, where there are four fine carvings featuring Sir Ywain at the castle gate, two dogs attacking a bear, a couple in a pew, and three seated angels under canopies (Fig.158 a, b, c, d).

(Fig 154) **St Peter, Alstonefield** *Box-pews.*

(Fig 155) **St Bartholomew, Blore** *Choir-stalls.*

(Fig 159) **St Mary, Enville**
*Misericords a. Sir Ywain at
the castle gate; b. two dogs
attacking a bear; c. a couple
in a pew; d. angels.*

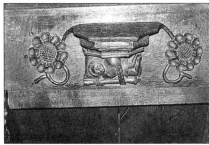

(Fig 156) **St Matthew, Walsall** *Misericord.*

(Fig 157) **St Matthew, Walsall** *Fifteenth-century
bench-end.*

(Fig 158) **St Mary, Enville** *Medieval choir-stall.*

Churches in the Regions of Staffordshire

Staffordshire is a large and varied county, and it has been thought best to group the remaining churches regionally, dividing the county into six areas, viz. the Northern Uplands, the Environs of the Potteries, the West, the Forest of Needwood, the South-east and the South-west.

The Northern Uplands

Alstonefield
Blore
Cheddleton
Horton
Ilam

Leek St Edward
Mayfield
Okeover
Rushton Spencer
Waterfall

The Staffordshire Moorlands are really an extension of the Peak District, and the finest scenery in the county is, as Henry Thorold has pointed out, often thought to be in Derbyshire. Leek is the administrative centre for this area, an attractive industrial town, with a fine medieval parish church dedicated to St Edward the Confessor and a Victorian church by Norman Shaw, built in 1885-87. Near to the Manifold and Dove valleys is a group of very rewarding churches, in lovely scenery: Alstonefield, Blore, Ilam, Mayfield, and Waterfall.

St Peter, Alstonefield

Alstonefield has an enviable situation in the finest scenery in Staffordshire, between the valleys of the Dove and Manifold. The village is attractive, and a great favourite with fell-walkers, while the church of St Peter (Fig.160) has some fine treasures.

The building is instructive because it incorporates elements from every period of medieval architecture. The oldest part of the church are some fragments of Anglo-Saxon crosses in the porch, tower and north aisle, similar to the crosses which may be seen at Ilam and Leek (q.v.).

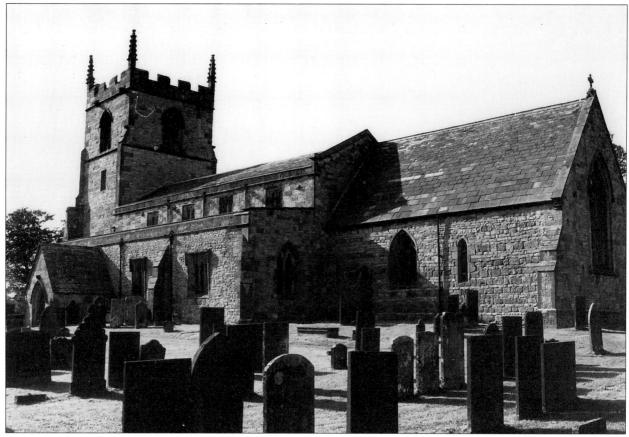

(Fig 160) **St Peter, Alstonefield**

(Fig 162) **St Peter, Alstonefield** *Norman chancel arch and Perpendicular arcades.*

Inside, the chancel arch dates from the Norman twelfth century (Fig.162). There are Early English lancet windows in the south aisle and chancel. The east window of the chancel is Decorated, and so are the main windows of the south aisle, although they are straight-headed (usually seen in the sixteenth century). Most of the rest of the building is Perpendicular – the arcades, clerestory and tower (Fig.161).

But good though the building is, it is the woodwork which is the real glory of St Peter's, especially the pulpit and pews. The pulpit is a magnificent two-decker, dating from 1637, finely carved (Fig.144, p67). Next to it is the Cotton family pew – a canopied structure, painted in a fairly ghastly grey-green. (The poet Charles Cotton lived in Beresford Hall, and entertained Izaak Walton, author of *The*

(Fig 161) **St Peter, Alstonefield**
Perpendicular tower.

Compleat Angler.) There are also a lectern, communion rail and a screen in the south aisle, all dating from the seventeenth century, together with an excellent set of box pews (Fig.154, p69).

Access: From Ashbourne, take the A515 towards Buxton; after about five miles, turn left for Alstonefield. The church is just to the south of the village centre.

St Bartholomew, Blore

St Bartholomew's deserves to be much better known, for it is a real treasure. Blore seems to mean 'bare hill' in the sense of a high, exposed place (Ekwall) and this is appropriate. There is now no village of Blore, only the former rectory and Blore Hall, long the home of the Bassett family.

The church (Fig.163) is built on rising ground behind the hall. The tower is Decorated (fourteenth century) with pinnacles and two-light windows with quatrefoils; most of the rest of the fabric is Perpendicular, apparently dating from as late as 1519, with a Perpendicular arcade and straight-headed 'Tudor' windows in the nave and chancel.

But although from the outside the church is lovely, it is the fittings, furnishing and monuments within that make it truly memorable. There is some excellent workwork, especially the late Perpendicular screen (Fig.141, p65) between the north aisle and the north chapel, with much intricate carving of unusual

character. On the south side of the nave there are box-pews, and in the chancel (Fig.151, p69) much panelling and notable choir-stalls (Fig.155, p70). Fragments of medieval glass are to be found in the south chancel window: in the right-hand light is portrayed St Anne teaching the Virgin Mary to read; in the left-hand light are two heads, one of a saint and the other of Christ crowned with thorns; this has been dated to 1519, and may have come from the workshop of Robert Power in Burton upon Trent (Marks).

The Bassett family, now extinct, lived at Blore Hall, and their memorials from the end of the fifteenth century to the first half of the seventeenth century are the show-pieces of the church. In the floor of the north aisle are brasses in memory of William Bassett II, who died in 1498, and his wife Joan. William's head is missing, but his wife's monument is complete and the costumes of each are said to be typical of the period. In the north aisle chapel is the gigantic sculptured alabaster monument to the last of the Bassetts, William Bassett VI. This complex assembly of figures was made by Jasper Hollemans at the behest of Judith, widow of William. In the centre, and at a higher elevation lies the recumbent figure of William, and on his right his son-in-law Henry Howard and on his left his wife Judith (Fig.127, p63). Behind Henry is the kneeling figure of the Bassetts' daughter Elizabeth, husband of Henry, and behind Judith is the Howards' daughter of the same name. The whole monument entirely fills the chapel, and is in need of some repair, but of its merit there is no doubt. The date of the

(Fig 163) **St Bartholomew, Blore**

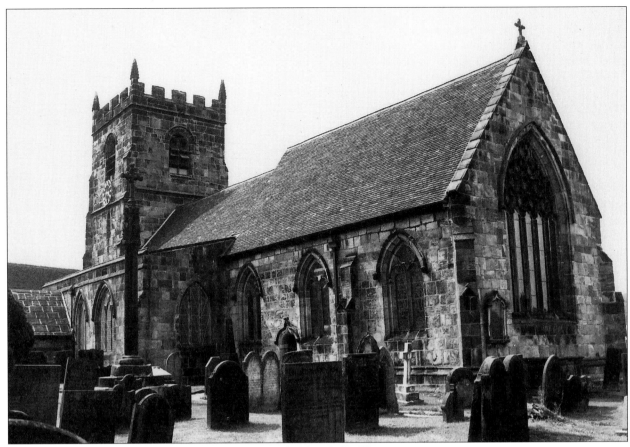

(Fig 164) **St Edward, Cheddleton**

monument is uncertain: William Bassett died in 1601 but his wife survived until 1640. Possibly the central figure of William Bassett was begun not long after his death, and the other figures added later.

Access: From Ashbourne, take the Leek road (A52) for five miles. At the crossroads where the A52 turns left for Stoke, and the A522 proceeds straight ahead for Leek, turn right into a lane which leads to Blore after 1½ miles. The church is on the right.

St Edward the Confessor, Cheddleton

Cheddleton is situated on the river Churnet, and the name means, appropriately enough, 'settlement in a narrow valley'. It is a place of some industrial historical importance, for it possesses an eighteenth-century flint mill, where flints from the south-east were brought by canal to be finely ground for use in the Potteries (Thorold); and at the time of writing of Pitt's History of Staffordshire (1817) 'vast quantities of limestone were conveyed from Caldon Low by the canal along the Churnet valley to Rocester and Uttoxeter'. There is also a Railway Museum at Cheddleton. The main road now bypasses the village centre; originally it crossed the Churnet by a ford, and climbed up the sunken Hollow Lane to the church, continuing to Stone by Ostlers Lane (Palliser).

So the parish church (Fig. 164) stands prominently on a hillside commanding wide views over the

surrounding countryside, and was originally a chapel-of-ease to the parish church in Leek; like the mother church it was dedicated to St Edward the Confessor. The church was probably founded early in the thirteenth century, shortly after the establishment of the Cistercian Abbey of Dieulacres in 1214. Such a date would fit in with the oldest part of the building, which is the Early English north arcade (Fig.165), supported by round piers and octagonal capitals. The south arcade, with octagonal piers, is Perpendicular, and so is the western tower. The best part of the church, however, is the Decorated chancel, where there is a fine east window with reticulated tracery. In the south wall of the chancel are an excellent set of sedilia and piscina in the Decorated style, with ogee headings and ball-flower decoration (Fig.166). The reredos is a fifteenth-century Flemish relief of the Deposition, with wings by William Morris (who was a friend of a churchwarden here). Also Flemish is the flamboyant brass lectern.

The Victorians, however, have also left their stamp on Cheddleton church, most notably in the stained glass, much of it designed by the Pre-Raphaelites Ford Madox Brown, Burne-Jones and D.G.Rosetti and executed by William Morris. The quality is high, especially the eight small figures designed by Madox Brown in the chancel. A further beautiful Burne-Jones window is in the south aisle.

Access: From Leek, go south along A520 towards Stone, and immediately after descending into the Churnet Valley and crossing the river, turn right up a

(Fig 165) **St Edward, Cheddleton** *The interior, looking east.*

(Fig 168) **St Michael, Horton** *The interior, looking east.*

(Fig 166) **St Edward, Cheddleton** *Piscina and sedilia with ball-flower decoration.*

steep hill to St Edward's, which is on the right. The key may be obtained at the butcher's shop opposite.

St Michael, Horton

Horton means 'settlement in a muddy place', which is rather surprising as the village is situated quite high up, in glorious and little-known countryside between Biddulph and Leek. Here is a lovely late Perpendicular church on a knoll, dedicated, as many hilltop churches are, to St Michael. Nearby is Horton Hall, a fine seventeenth-century dwelling; Dairy House Farm and Harracles Hall are other distinguished buildings in the vicinity.

St Michael's (Fig.167) was originally a chapel-of-ease to Leek, and remained so until 1450. At about this time, the north aisle was added to the pre-existing church, and this is now the oldest part of the present building. Most of the rest of the church was probably built in the first half of the sixteenth century, and is therefore late Perpendicular. The west tower has eight pinnacles, and the south aisle is battlemented (Fig.43, p26). The windows are straight-headed (so-called Tudor windows) in both chancel and aisles. Inside, the north arcade is

Perpendicular, the south being added in 1864, together with the east window. The roof of the nave has four trusses with cambered tie-beams, and is original (Fig.168). The attractive screen is Victorian, carved by an incumbent, the Reverend Bennet Blakeway. There are monuments to the Wedgwoods, who lived at Harracles; they first came to Horton in the fourteenth century. The earliest is a brass to John Wedgwood (died 1589) and later marble tablets to descendants of the same name who died in 1724 and 1757.

Access: From Leek, take the A523 towards Macclesfield, and after 1½ miles turn left into B5331; after half-a-mile, at a T-junction turn left. Take two right forks, and the road climbs steadily towards Horton village. St Michael's is then up a steep hill on the right.

Holy Cross, Ilam

Ilam might well be regarded as the finest estate village in the county, with attractive houses clustered around the cross erected in 1840 in memory of the deceased wife of Jesse Watts Russell – a conscious re-enactment of the Eleanor Crosses built by Edward I in the late thirteenth century. The church and the hall (built in 1821) share an enviable position in a loop of the River

(Fig 167) **St Michael, Horton**

(Fig 169) **Holy Cross, Ilam** *David Pike Watts memorial, by Sir Francis Chantrey (1831).*

Manifold (the name Ilam comes from Hyle, an old name for the Manifold) as it winds its way towards the Dove. The land around is now maintained as a country park by the National Trust.

At first glance, the church appears Victorian (Fig. 3, p8), and indeed much of the fabric dates from the rebuilding of 1855; in addition, there is the octagonal mausoleum to the north, dating from 1831, about which perhaps the less said the better. But the aspect from the south is fine, with the saddle-back tower seen against the backdrop of rolling hills. There are indications of earlier building, too: a blocked Saxon doorway, an Early English lancet window in the tower, and the south chapel of 1618, a rare date for church building, and still showing straight-headed 'Tudor' windows in the Jacobean era. In the churchyard are two Anglo-Saxon crosses (see p11); a third can be seen on the walk along the north bank of the Manifold, just past the hall.

Inside there is much to see: the chapel of St Bertelin, the Meverell monument, the Pike Watts statue and, above all, the font. The chapel contains the shrine of St Bertelin, a little-known saint from the eighth century who lived as a hermit on an island on the River Sow near Stafford (see p42). The shrine consists of the base only, with large quatrefoils around the sides. Also in this chapel are the two alabaster effigies of Robert Meverell and his wife (1626) and, in a wall-monument behind, their daughter Lady Cromwell, kneeling,with her four children (Fig. 129, p62). The Meverells lived at Throwley Hall, two miles up the Manifold Valley and now ruinous.

The octagonal mausoleum contains the celebrated family group of David Pike Watts (Fig. 169) blessing his daughter and her three children. This is by

Chantrey (1831): the daughter was the first wife of Jesse Watts Russell, whose memorial cross in the village has already been mentioned. The statue is described by Pevsner as 'theatrical . . .but not at all without feeling', and by Esdaile as 'bad melodrama'. The observer must make his/her judgement, but I rather like it.

The finest artefact at Ilam, however, is undoubtedly the tub font, which is late Saxon or early Norman (Fig.93, p50). The carving is lively, with human figures and beasts separated by arcades.

Access: From Ashbourne, take the A515 northwards, and after one mile turn left for Thorpe. From Thorpe, descend into Dovedale, and then after crossing the river, the road leads to Ilam. The church is a quarter of a mile beyond the village, on the left.

St Edward the Confessor, Leek

Leek is the major centre of the north of the county, and is a small industrial yet attractive town. It is presided over by the parish church (Fig.170), built prominently on a hill and dedicated to St Edward the Confessor, King of England from 1042-1066. From these times date the two Saxon crosses in the churchyard (see p12).

There must have been a Norman church in Leek, but this was destroyed by fire in 1297. It was replaced by

(Fig 171) **St Edward the Confessor, Leek** *The south rose window.*

the present largely Decorated church early in the fourteenth century. The most striking external features of the building are the large rose windows (Fig.171) in what used to be the north and south transepts and the intersecting tracery of the east window of the north aisle. The west tower is also fourteenth century, though crowned with a later Perpendicular top replete with pinnacles.

The interior is dominated by the enormous western gallery (Fig. 172), which rises tier upon tier to the hammerbeam roof (Fig. 173). The great virtue of the gallery is that it enables the visitor to have a really

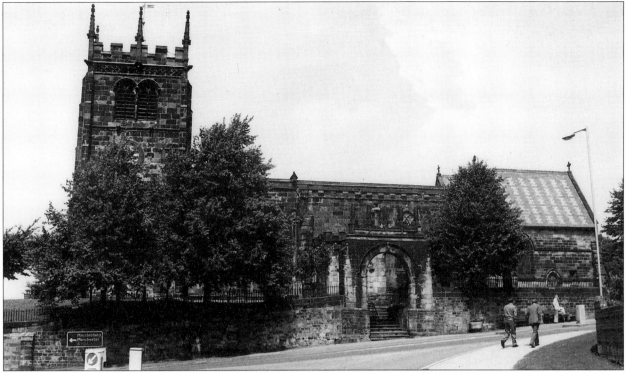

(Fig 170) **St Edward the Confessor, Leek**

(Fig 172) **St Edward the Confessor, Leek** *The Western gallery and panelled and embossed roof.*

(Fig 173) **St Edward the Confessor, Leek** *Early sixteenth-century roof.*

(Fig 174) **St John the Baptist, Mayfield** *Norman arcade and Decorated chancel.*

close inspection of the roof, which is panelled and decorated by bosses at the intersection of the timbers. The arcades, in contrast, are not impressive and are short, limited only to three arches at the eastern end of the nave. The chancel is largely Victorian, dating from a restoration of 1865-67. Both the pulpit and the font are also of this period, but are not without character. Note the fine sixteenth-century brass to the Ashenhurst family in the east wall of the north aisle.

Access: St Edward's is on the A523 (Macclesfield road) just to the north of the town centre.

St John the Baptist, Mayfield

Mayfield is known as 'Medevelde' in Domesday Book, and this apparently means 'the field where madder grows' (Ekwall) – madder being a plant whose root yielded a red dye which was used for cloth and was also used medicinally in medieval times as a treatment for amenorrhoea. Other authorities say that the name was originally Maethelfield – meaning 'meeting field' – such is the uncertainty which often surrounds ancient place-names. Whatever its early name, the village has an enviable situation in the valley of the Dove, on the borders of Derbyshire and Staffordshire, and its church is superb.

The basic structure is twelfth-century Norman, with a fine south arcade of semicircular arches (Fig.174) supported by cylindrical piers bearing capitals showing scallop and leaf carving (Figs.14, p13 and 27, p18); the north arcade is a little later, still showing semicircular arches but the piers are quatrefoil in cross-section and bear different capitals. The south doorway is also Norman, and has one order of colonettes, with three-dimensional zigzags and pellet

  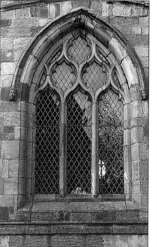 

(Fig 175) **St John the Baptist, Mayfield** *Windows: left to right, Y tracery; Intersecting tracery; Reticulated tracery; Perpendicular.*

decoration in the arch. The door, with original ironwork, is also notable.

There is an instructive series of windows of the late thirteenth century and early fourteenth century (Fig.175); in the south aisle is one with Y-tracery (the end of the Early English period) and another shows intersecting tracery (early Decorated). The east window of the chancel has reticulated tracery of the later Decorated period. The chancel is in fact

(Fig 176) **St John the Baptist, Mayfield** *Communion rail, c.1660.*

remarkable for its length and width. Its most memorable feature is the three-sided communion rail made of oak in 1660 (Fig.176, and Fig.153, p69) showing excellent carving. The pulpit, altar table and benches date form 1630-33. The font, at the west end of the nave, is a handsome octagonal piece, dated 1514.

The west tower (Fig.177) is Perpendicular, with a Perpendicular window, (Fig.175) built in 1515 and bearing eight pinnacles. The west door still shows the bullet-holes fired by Prince Charles Edward's troops when they went rampaging through the village in 1745. The south porch was built last of all, in the early seventeenth century.

Access: From Ashbourne, take the A52 towards Leek; after just over a mile, and immediately after crossing the Dove and entering Staffordshire, turn left on to B5031. Take the first turning on the left, and the church will be found after half-a-mile on the right-hand side.

All Saints, Okeover

Okeover means 'the slope (or bank) where oaks grow', and indeed Okeover is situated just above the Dove where it forms the boundary between Staffordshire and Derbyshire. The manor of Okeover is very ancient, being mentioned in Domesday Book; it was granted to Orm (is this the same Orm who founded the Norman church of St Chad at Stafford?), a tenant of

(Fig 177) **St John the Baptist, Mayfield** *Perpendicular west tower.*

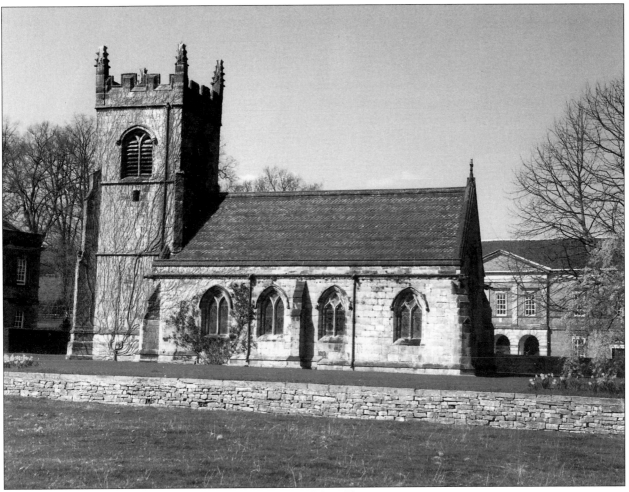

(Fig 178) **All Saints, Okeover**

Tutbury Priory at some time between 1094 and 1113 (Palliser) and his family continued to hold Okeover in the direct male line for 850 years. The church at Okeover was apparently founded by Burton Abbey as a chapelry of Ilam. At some later time, it became a parish church in its own right, and the advowson was acquired by the Okeover family. The church stands very close to the hall, which was built by Leak Okeover in the eighteenth century; the present owner is Capt. Sir Peter Walker-Okeover, whose family now

(Fig 179) **All Saints, Okeover** *Monument to Leak and Mary Okeover by Joseph Wilton (1765).*

maintains the church, which is not open to the public and which is no longer used for public worship. Sir Peter tells me that the church is designated as a 'peculiar', in that the house is the parish; it is believed that there are only four similar churches in the country.

All Saints' church has a delectable setting, in parkland close to the hall (Fig.178), and just half-a-mile from the River Dove. The building is basically of the fourteenth century, though much restored. There is a variety of Decorated windows, progressing from Y-tracery in the nave to reticulated tracery in the north and south windows of the chancel, and flowing tracery in the east window. The chancel windows contain some attractive panels of fourteenth-century stained glass. There is a sixteenth-century brass to Humphrey Okeover. But the greatest treasure of the church is the fine monument by Joseph Wilton to Leak and Mary Okeover (1765); above the rectangular inscribed tablet is the reclining figure of an angel holding a wreath and an inverted torch of life before an urn on a pedestal, with a medallion of the husband and wife (Fig.179).

St Lawrence, Rushton Spencer

This is a difficult church to find, and even more difficult to get inside, but it is so enchanting that the effort is well worth while. St Lawrence's stands alone

(Fig 180) **St Lawrence, Rushton Spencer**

(Fig 181) **St Lawrence, Rushton Spencer** *The studded oak door (1713).*

(Fig 182) **St Lawrence, Rushton Spencer** *The interior, looking west.*

on a hilltop, commanding extensive views of the undulating country on the Cheshire/Staffordshire border between Leek and Macclesfield. Until 1865, it was a chapel-of-ease to Leek.

Timber-framed churches are rare: Morris reckoned that there were only 27 in England; eight are in Cheshire, two in Shropshire, and there are two in Staffordshire – Betley (q.v.) and Rushton Spencer. Most of the rest are in Essex.

Timber-framed buildings are hard to date but the woodwork is presumably medieval; the original building was probably all half-timbered, like Marton in Cheshire, but the exterior was rebuilt in stone at some time in the seventeenth century. The quaint dormer windows in the roof were added in 1842 (Fig. 180). The splendidly studded oak door bears the date 1713 (Fig. 181), and above the east window is the date 1690. A weather-boarded bell turret sits astride the saddleback roof.

The interior is a maze of woodwork (Fig. 182); two heavy tie-beams secure the timber roof, and one of these supports the west gallery. The oak posts separating the nave from the north aisle were originally part of the timber-framing of the medieval

(Fig 183) **St James and St Bartholomew, Waterfall.**

church. At the east end, there is a seventeenth-century pulpit, with an enclosed family pew, a Royal Arms of the reign of Queen Anne, hatchments and Commandments board. The stone font is bonded into the west wall, and is clearly of great antiquity.

Access: From Leek, take the A523 north towards Macclesfield. Rushton Spencer lies about one mile beyond Rudyard Reservoir. In the village, turn left, then take a left fork and climb steeply up a narrow lane to the top of the hill; a track on the left leads across a field to the church.

St James and St Bartholomew, Waterfall

The village takes its name from the behaviour of the river Hamps, which in summer may suddenly disappear among lime-stone rocks near here, and follow a subterranean course for a while on its way to join the Manifold.

Waterfall is one of those churches for which one is utterly unprepared. It makes a pretty sight across the meadows near to the village (Fig.183), but the exterior does not really make one expect great things inside. The building looks late eighteenth century or later, and

(Fig 184) **St James and St Bartholomew, Waterfall** *The Norman chancel arch.*

indeed it is. The nave has large Venetian windows, and the tower was built in 1792. The chancel, too, looks Georgian, although in fact it was built in 1890, using older masonry.

But step inside, and quite unexpectedly one enters the twelfth century. The south doorway is Norman, but is eclipsed by the most impressive Norman chancel arch (Fig.184), decorated with chevron, with saltire crosses in the hoodmould above. The seventeenth century also contributes, with some fine Jacobean panelling and communion rails, also a Jacobean screen with balusters.

Access: From Leek, take the Ashbourne road (A522) for about six miles. Just before entering Waterhouses, the turning to Waterfall leads off to the left. The church is in fields, just past the crossroads in Waterfall.

The Environs of the Potteries

Audley
Betley
Bradley-in-the-Moors
Checkley
Denstone (see p36.)
Draycott-in-the-Moors
Leigh
Madeley
Sandon
Stone
Stowe-by-Chartley
Swynnerton

The churches of the Potteries themselves are not in general of great interest to the visitor but all around the Five Towns, and within easy reach of them, are village churches, some of outstanding quality.

St James, Audley

Audley is an industrial village on the edge of the Potteries, six miles north-west of Newcastle-under-Lyme, and was the scene of the area's worst mining disaster in 1918, when 155 men died at Halmer End. But the settlement is ancient, and is mentioned in Domesday Book. The Audley family acquired the manor and estate in the thirteenth century.

The first half of the fourteenth century is the Decorated period of medieval church architecture; Audley church is largely of this time and contains some excellent monuments of the same period. The sturdy west tower (Fig.185) stands imposingly above the village street, and one passes through the west door into the long nave; this is lit by a Victorian clerestorey.

But the main attraction is the chancel, and the chancel arch is exceptionally high (Fig.186). The very attractive east window is apparently Victorian. The Decorated sedilia and piscina on the south wall of the chancel are very fine, and just before them is a brass in the floor to Sir Thomas de Audley (1385, Fig.187), who had his seat nearby at Heighley Castle. In the north wall of the chancel is the stone effigy of a knight, identified as Sir John Delves; his legs are uncrossed and rest on a dog (Fig.103, p54). He was squire to Lord Audley at the battle of Poitiers (1356) when the Black Prince captured the king of France. Nearby is the recumbent effigy of Edward Vernon, vicar of Audley (1622). Also on the north wall of the chancel is a further brass to William Abnett (1628).

Access: From M6, junction 16, take the A500 eastwards towards Newcastle for just over a mile, and then turn south for Audley. At the T-junction in Audley, turn left and then right for St James'.

(Fig 185) **St James, Audley** *Decorated west tower.*

(Fig 186) **St James, Audley** *East window, chancel arch, and arcades.*

(Fig 187) **St James, Audley** *Brass of Sir Thomas de Audley (1385).*

St Margaret, Betley

Betley, in the north-west of the county near the border with Cheshire, is an attractive village with some good houses. It was formerly a place of some importance, being a market town, and in the thirteenth century the site of the first recorded fulling mill in Staffordshire.

St Margaret's is unusual in that it is one of the two timber-framed churches in Staffordshire (see p80). The exterior is not appealing, having suffered much restoration in the nineteenth century, though the chancel dates from 1610 and the tower was rebuilt in 1711. The interior, however, is remarkable and rewarding. The timber arcades (Figs.188, 189) are supported by octagonal piers of Spanish chestnut from which arise arched braces which, with tie-beams, support the timbers of the roof. What is the date of these arcades? Timbered buildings are notoriously hard to date, but the arcades are almost certainly pre-Reformation. The timbers of the clerestory, however, are Victorian.

There is more good woodwork to see: a Perpendicular parclose screen with single light divisions defines the north chapel, and there is a fine

(Fig 188) **St Margaret, Betley** *The timber arcades, looking east.*

(Fig 189) **St Margaret, Betley** *The arcades, looking west.*

Jacobean pulpit with two tiers of blank arcading which originally contained scenes from the life of Christ (Fig. 145, p66). The monument on the north wall of the chancel is to Ralph Egerton and his wife (1610) and depicts two figures kneeling on cushions on either side of a prayer desk, facing each other and flanked by shields and columns; their son built the chancel. Jeavons (1955-56) attributed this monument to the workshop of Jasper Hollemans in Burton upon Trent.

Access: From junction 16 of the M6, take the A500 towards Nantwich, and at the second roundabout turn left onto A531. Betley is two miles along this road; the church is along a lane on the left.

St Leonard, Bradley-in-the-Moors

Bradley, west of Stafford (p93) means 'broad meadow' (Bradelea in Domesday Book), but this Bradley means 'wood where boards were got' (Bretlei in Domesday Book – Ekwall). Bradley-in-the-Moors

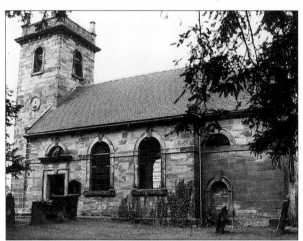

(Fig 190) **St Leonard, Bradley-in-the-Moors**

is described by Thorold as 'a delectable spot in high country above the Churnet valley, with views of Alton Castle', and for those who love simple, unspoiled, peaceful churches, St Leonard's is a treasure.

Most of the notable Georgian churches in Staffordshire are urban, but here is a rural one, a perfect plain little church built in 1750, and not altered since (Figs. 190, 191). There is just a west tower, nave

(Fig 191) **St Leonard, Bradley-in-the-Moors** *The plain Georgian interior.*

and chancel, and inside are the Hanoverian Royal Arms. The windows of nave and chancel are arched, and above the doorways are semicircular windows.

Access: From the Uttoxeter Road out of Cheadle, turn into B5032 towards Ashbourne. After nearly two miles turn right for Bradley-in-the-Moors, and the church is on the left. Entrance to the church is through a gate by a cottage (whence the key may be obtained); the path on the right goes to the church.

St Mary and All Saints, Checkley

Checkley, in the Tean Valley, is clearly an ancient settlement; known in Domesday Book as Cedla, it goes back even further to Anglo-Saxon times for in the churchyard are the remains of Saxon crosses (see Fig. 9, p11).

The church (Fig. 192), thought by some to be the finest in north Staffordshire, is rewarding and rather complex. From the outside, the strikingly elegant chancel is replete with windows showing intersecting tracery (Fig.35, p22) from the Decorated age (first half of the fourteenth century). An unusual feature is the presence of rosettes at some of the junctions of the tracery. The aisles shows Perpendicular windows on the north side, and straight-headed so-called Tudor windows on the south and in the clerestory; these in fact date from a rebuilding early in the seventeenth century. The south doorway is early fourteenth-century; it has three orders of columns, and is adorned with ball-flower, a typical Decorated motif. The west tower appears to be Decorated below and Perpendicular above.

Within, the two arcades are very different (Fig.193). The north arcade is Early English; the much taller south arcade appears to be late Norman, but probably rebuilt and heightened (Pevsner). The roof of the nave is panelled, and of low pitch; like the clerestory, it dates from the early seventeenth century. At the west end of the nave, the unusual font (Fig.92, p50) shows a donkey flanked by palm-trees; it has been variously described as Norman or Saxon/Danish.

The chancel is distinguished – reminiscent of the fine Decorated chancels of Derbyshire. It is spacious, tall and light, with fine intersecting tracery in the windows. There is some excellent stained glass dating

(Fig 192) **St Mary, Checkley**

(Fig 193) **St Mary, Checkley** *Intersecting tracery in the east window; north arcade (left) is Early English; south arcade (right) late Norman, probably rebuilt.*

from about 1300 in the east window; the lower scenes show, from north to south, the martyrdom of St Stephen, the sacrifice of Isaac, the Crucifixion, St Margaret and the dragon, and the murder of Thomas a'Becket in Canterbury Cathedral; above are various saints. In the south chancel window, some interesting roundels depict agricultural scenes; these appear to have come from the former medieval rectory during the incumbency of Anthony Draycott (1535-60) (Marks); possibly they may be of Flemish origin. Sixteenth-century choir-stalls may be seen in the south side of the chancel.

Croxden Abbey, a Cistercian foundation of the twelfth century, was situated four miles from Checkley; the abbey was dissolved in 1538, and

Thomas Chawner, the last abbot, died six years later and his worn grave-slab may be seen in the chancel at Checkley. Just to the south is the magnificent alabaster tomb-chest of Godfrey and Margaret Foljambe, who sequestrated the abbey. So, as has been pointed out in the excellent church guide, the sequestrated and sequestrator of Croxden Abbey lie side by side.

Access: Checkley is midway between Cheadle and Uttoxeter (A522). The church is just off the main road, on the south side. A notice informs visitors where the key may be obtained.

St Margaret, Draycott-in-the-Moors

St Margaret's is pleasantly situated on the outskirts of the Potteries, on a low hill on the north side of the Roman road leading from Derventio to Chesterton (now the A50). The oldest part of the building is the lower part of the west tower (Fig.194), where a window with Y-tracery betrays its early thirteenth-century origin. The north chapel, containing the tombs, came later in the thirteenth century, and the rest of the church was largely rebuilt in Victorian times.

But it is the interest and quality of the monuments that draws most visitors to St Margaret's. In the north chapel are six monuments ranging from *c.*1300 to 1662, all but the oldest commemorating members of the Draycott family. The earliest effigy is a stone figure of an unknown knight clad in chainmail (Fig.99, p52), armed with a half-drawn sword, with his legs crossed. There are five Draycott monuments: (1) the tomb of Philip and Elizabeth Draycott, the finest

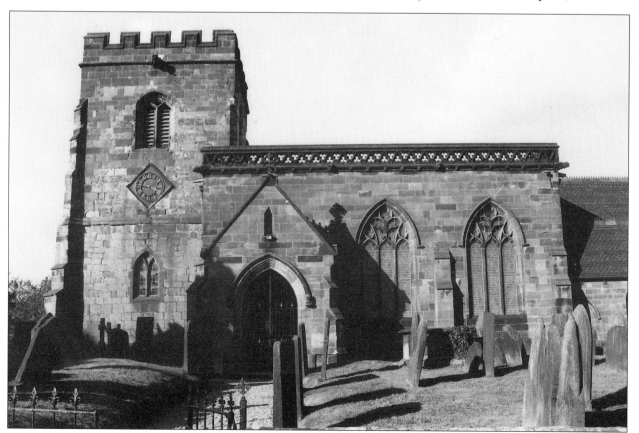

(Fig 194) **St Margaret, Draycott-in-the-Moors**

(Fig 195) **All Saints, Leigh**

(Fig.111, p56) from the Royley workshop in Burton upon Trent (1559); (2) Richard and Alice Draycott (1544); (3) Philip Draycott (1604); (4) John and Elizabeth Draycott (1607; Fig. 121, p60); and (5) Richard Draycott (1662). Just outside the Draycott chapel is a wall-monument to Sir William Draycott, rector of the church, who died in 1512.

The Draycotts lived in Paynsley Hall, about a mile to the south of the church. Dr Anthony Draycott was rector from 1535, and during the reign of Mary I, pursued the Protestants with zeal. After the accession of Queen Elizabeth, he was committed to prison for a while, finally ending his days in 1570 at Paynsley Hall. The family remained Catholics until the estate passed out of their hands in 1698; and like the Giffards at Chillington and the Fitzherberts at Swynnerton provided 'gentry protection' to many of their tenants during the years when Catholics were persecuted.

Access: From Stoke-on-Trent, take the A50 towards Uttoxeter, continuing through Blythe Bridge after the A50 diverges to the right. Draycott is a mile after the road to Cheadle leaves on the left; St Margaret's will be seen on higher ground to the left of the main road.

All Saints, Leigh

The village of Leigh is set in pastoral country between Cheadle and Uttoxeter, not far from the river Blithe; and the Bagot family of Blithfield have long had extensive estates here. In 1845, the medieval church of Leigh was replaced at the expense of the Bagots by the

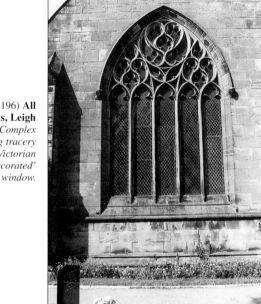

(Fig 196) **All Saints, Leigh** *Complex flowing tracery in this Victorian 'Decorated' window.*

present astonishing building, which was designed by a little-known architect, Thomas Johnson of Lichfield. The result is a stunning church – the most perfect Victorian representation of Decorated architecture.

The church (Fig.195) commands an extensive view to the south over the Blithe valley, and is cruciform in shape. The windows show complex flowing tracery (Fig.196), the tower battlemented, without pinnacles. Inside, the nave has arcades of five bays, with piers of unusual shape and carved capitals (Fig.197). Both the

(Fig 197) **All Saints, Leigh**
The south arcade and chancel arch.

crossing and the chancel have stone rib vaulting – a rare feature in a parish church of any era (Fig.198). The tiling of the chancel floor is said to have been designed by Pugin. There is some medieval stained glass in the chancel, and some Victorian glass by Morris, Burne-Jones and others. A fine alabaster tomb of Sir John Ashenhurst (1520) is in the south transept. The font is fourteenth-century, with quatrefoils.

Access: From Uttoxeter, take the A522 north-westwards towards Cheadle; at Fole, turn left, and pass under the A50; then turn right and later left for Church Leigh. All Saints' church is on the right.

(Fig 198) **All Saints, Leigh** *The vaulted chancel.*

All Saints, Madeley

Madeley is a large village on the outskirts of the Potteries, just to the west of the M6. The road from Newcastle meanders through Madeley Heath, Little Madeley, and Middle Madeley, and then expectations are raised by the pool and the Old Hall, once the seat

(Fig 200) **All Saints, Madeley** *The arcades – north late Norman (Transitional); south Perpendicular.*

of John Offley, friend of Izaak Walton and dedicatee of *The Compleat Angler.* Then round the next corner on the left is All Saints church (Fig.199) somewhat over-restored, but unmistakably (except for the chancel) a medieval building.

The interior is rather dark but has some fine features to interest the visitor. The north arcade is late Norman, with octagonal piers and many-scalloped capitals (Fig.200) said by Pevsner to be rare. Most of the rest

(Fig 199) **All Saints, Madeley**

(Fig 201) **All Saints, Sandon**

of the church – the south arcade, the transepts and the tower are Perpendicular, the chancel Victorian. The tower gallery dates from 1635.

In the north transept is a table tomb to Randolph and Isabella Egerton (1522) with an incised alabaster slab on the top and figurines under canopies around the sides (Fig.106, p56). Note also the sixteenth-century brasses in the floor of the south transept to John Egerton and his wife. There is a Perpendicular screen (Fig.142, p66). The pulpit is Jacobean, with two tiers of blank arches, the panels having been painted in gold by (it is said) D.G.Rossetti. Also from the pre-Raphaelites is the striking stained glass of the west window in the south aisle: this has been ascribed to William Morris and Sir Edward Burne-Jones.

Access: From Newcastle-under-Lyme, take the A525 towards Whitchurch. Madeley church is on the left, one mile after passing under the M6.

All Saints, Sandon

This delightful church stands alone and imposingly on a bluff overlooking the Trent Valley (Fig.201). It is now an estate church, the village having been moved half-a-mile away at some time in the sixteenth or seventeenth century.

The church is replete with memorials to members of the various families who have held the local manor. After the Norman Conquest the manor was given to the Earl of Chester. From him it passed to William de Malbanc, whose son gave the church to the monks of

Combermere Abbey in Cheshire. The manor later passed by marriage to the Staffords of Stafford Castle, and then, again by marriage, to the Erdeswick family in 1338, remaining in their hands until the death of Sampson Erdeswick in 1603. He was a noted antiquary, and wrote the first history of Staffordshire. His stepson, George Digby, then bought the estate from Sampson's son Richard. Digby's daughter and heiress brought the estate to Lord Gerard by marriage, and later it passed, again by marriage, to the Dukes of Hamilton. In 1777, the estate was bought by the first Baron Harrowby, whose descendants still live in Sandon Hall.

Nothing remains of the Norman church which was presumably built in the twelfth century, and the oldest part of the present building is the south aisle which was built as the nave in the thirteenth century in the Early English style, the windows showing Y-tracery. Around 1300 the chancel was built, and a new nave was also constructed (Fig.202), the previous nave becoming the present south aisle. A shorter north aisle followed in the fourteenth century, with windows showing Decorated flowing tracery of rather an unusual pattern. Lastly, in the fifteenth century, the Perpendicular tower was built into the existing south and west walls.

The great interest of Sandon church, however, is not so much the architecture but the furnishings and the monuments. The interior is dominated by the remodelled screen, which incorporates some originally Perpendicular tracery; above it is a gallery (Fig.203) which is the family pew of the Earls of

(Fig 202) **All Saints, Sandon** *Nave and arch-braced roof.*

(Fig 203) **All Saints, Sandon** *The Harrowby family's gallery pew above the screen (1782).*

angles; it is dated 1669, but looks a lot older. There is some excellent seventeenth-century woodwork: the pulpit (Fig.148, p68), complete with tester above, is very fine, and so are some of the benches and pews in the chancel.

The chancel is dominated by the enormous monument to Sampson Erdeswick; he lies recumbent, with his two wives kneeling against the wall above him (Fig.119, p59). The whole monument is surmounted by an imposing but not particularly beautiful superstructure. Earlier members of the Erdeswick family are commemorated by four tombs on top of which lie incised alabaster slabs; the sides of the tombs are decorated with heraldic shields; there are two tombs on the north wall of the chancel and two on the south. Above the first tomb on the north wall is a painted window, on either side of which are painted the genealogical trees of the Erdeswick family. Also in the chancel is the white marble monument to George Digby.

Access: From Stafford, take the A518 eastwards towards Uttoxeter, and after three miles turn left on to A51 at Weston. Two miles later, turn right along a lane which climbs towards Sandon church, on the edge of Sandon Park.

St Michael, Stone

St Michael's, Stone, is a good example of an eighteenth-century town church. Although aptly described by Thorold as 'a large formal preaching box', this perhaps does not quite do justice to St

Harrowby. The fine roof timbers, consisting of arched braces, can be well seen from this gallery, and are accompanied by the Stuart Royal Arms and the Harrowby family hatchments. The north aisle was adapted in 1851 to serve as the Harrowby chapel, and contains an unusual square font with four figures at the

(Fig 204) **St Michael, Stone**

(Fig 205) **St Michael, Stone** *The interior, with side-galleries and box-pews.*

Michael's. It is indeed a mid-eighteenth century building, designed by William Robinson, and built between 1753 and 1758. It has a nice situation in the town, with a spacious churchyard, and the exterior (Fig.204) is remarkable mainly for the windows. These are not the large 'Venetian' windows characteristic of many churches of this period but instead show Y-tracery reminiscent of the thirteenth century – i.e an unusually early example of Gothic revival. The west tower is handsome, battlemented with pinnacles.

The interior is very attractive, with side-galleries on wooden supports, and box-pews (Fig.205). The chancel was altered in the nineteenth century, and provided with a pseudo-Perpendicular east window.

Access: From Stafford, take the A34 north towards Stoke-on-Trent. After 5 miles, the A51 joins this road at a roundabout; continue to the next roundabout, then turn right for Stone. At the T-junction with the Lichfield road, St Michael's will be seen straight ahead.

St John the Baptist, Stowe-By-Chartley

The ruins of Chartley Castle stand imposingly to the west of the main Stafford-to-Uttoxeter road. In the Elizabethan hall nearby (now destroyed) Mary Queen of Scots was imprisoned in 1586, and was transferred from there to her last place of captivity, Fotheringhay. About a mile to the south of the castle is the pleasant village of Stowe-by-Chartley, graced by the church of St John the Baptist (Fig.206). Chartley itself is one of Staffordshire's deserted villages.

The church's origins are clearly Norman, as evidenced by the splendid south doorway (Fig.207), which shows weathered scallop capitals and much zigzag decoration in the arches. The church was enlarged in the fourteenth century, the chancel being lengthened and the west tower built (probably replacing an earlier one). The east window in the chancel, and the south windows of the nave show simple Decorated tracery, as do the belfry windows of the tower. In 1866, the chancel was reconstructed, and the Norman-looking chancel arch dates from this time, as does the north aisle.

In the north wall of the chancel is the showpiece of the church, the tomb of Sir Walter Devereux, later

(Fig 206) **St John, Stowe-by-Chartley**

(Fig 207) **St John, Stowe-by-Chartley** *The fine Norman south doorway.*

(Fig 209) **St Mary, Swynnerton** *The interior, looking east.*

Viscount Hereford, and his two wives (Fig.109, p56). He served Henry VIII well in his French wars, and was admitted to the Order of the Garter. He married Anne, the last Baroness of Chartley and died in 1558. On the tomb-chest lie three recumbent effigies, and round the sides of the tomb are well-carved figurines and early Renaissance decoration. In the chancel, note also the tablets commemorating General Sir Walter Congreve and his son William, both of whom were awarded the Victoria Cross.

Access: From Stafford, take the Uttoxeter Road (A518), and about one mile after crossing the A51 a road on the right leads to Stowe-by-Chartley. In the village, turn left at the crossroads for the church.

(Fig 208) **St Mary, Swynnerton**

St Mary, Swynnerton

As already mentioned (p50) Swynnerton church is the fortunate possessor of a magnificent thirteenth-century statue of Christ. But St Mary's has more to offer the discerning visitor. It is a pleasant estate village, and Swynnerton Hall is the seat of Lord Stafford. The family remained Catholic after the Reformation, and many of their tenants adhered to the old religion. As a result, two churches, St Mary's (Fig.208) and the Catholic church of Our Lady of the Assumption, stand opposite each other, adjacent to Swynnerton Hall, the whole forming a most attractive grouping.

There is evidence of Norman workmanship at St Mary's: the west doorway in the tower is Norman, and so also is an inner doorway in the tower leading to the nave. Here the arch above the door shows prominent beak-head and pellet decoration, in a better state of preservation than is usual as they have not been exposed to the elements. Inside (Fig. 209), Early English arcades separate the aisles from the nave, and the chancel is also of this period. The east window is a little later, with reticulated tracery of the Decorated age (first half of the fourteenth century). In the south wall of the chancel are a defaced piscina and sedilia. The Perpendicular chapel to the south of the chancel houses the statue of Christ (Fig.96, p50) and the upper part of the tower is also Perpendicular, with a frieze below the parapet and gargoyles at the corners and sides.

Access: From Junction 16 of the M6, take the A519 south towards Eccleshall. At the junction with the A51, turn left, and after a quarter of a mile, right for Swynnerton, where St Mary's will be seen on the left.

The West

Ashley
Blymhill
Bradley
Broughton (see p29)
Chebsey
Church Eaton
Coppenhall (see p19)
Eccleshall (see p20)
Forton
Gnosall (see p39)
High Offley

Ingestre (see p30)
Lapley
Norbury
Penkridge (see p40)
Seighford
Stafford St Chad (see p16)
Stafford St Mary (see p42)
Weston-under-Lizard

West of the M6, the countryside undulates gently towards the Shropshire border. This is pastoral Staffordshire, largely unmarred by industry, still mainly rural and agricultural, with peaceful villages, winding canals and some lovely churches.

In the Middle Ages, it was dominated ecclesiastically by Eccleshall, the seat for many centuries of the Bishops of Lichfield.

St John the Baptist, Ashley

This part of Staffordshire was originally heavily wooded, as the name implies: 'ley' being derived from the Anglo-Saxon 'leah', a clearing in woodland (Palliser). A church has stood on the present site at least since the thirteenth century, but the present building, apart from the tower, is Victorian. The tower is said to date from the fourteenth century, but what one sees today was mostly built around 1612.

By the mid-nineteenth century, the church was 'ruinous', and the building was demolished, except for the tower, and replaced by the present structure, designed by J.Ashdown (1860-62). At the west end of the nave, the former gallery was extended forwards to accommodate the new organ, the carved and decorated underside of this loft forming the rear ceiling of the nave (Fig.210). Over the chancel arch is a black basalt funeral urn made by Josiah Wedgwood in

memory of the third Viscount Chetwynd. Separating the nave from the chancel is the richly carved rood-screen, with the figures of Christ on the cross, flanked by the Virgin Mary and St John; this dates from 1910, as does the elaborate reredos to the altar.

There are numerous monuments in Ashley church, but the showpiece is undoubtedly the huge Gerard monument to the north of the chancel, said by Betjeman to be the largest Elizabethan monument in any English parish church. Whether it should really be regarded as Elizabethan is a moot point: it commemorates Sir Gilbert Gerard, who died in 1592, but the monument was apparently not erected until about 1612, at the expense of Sir Gilbert's son Thomas, Lord Gerard. It is thought to be the work of Jasper Hollemans of Burton upon Trent (see p56). It shows lifesize figures of Sir Gilbert and his wife lying side by side, with their two sons kneeling, one at their head and the other at their feet, the four daughters being carved in relief at the back (Fig.120, p59).

Access: From Newcastle-under-Lyme, take the A53 westwards towards Market Drayton. One mile after crossing the A51, turn left for Ashley. The church is at a crossroads in the village.

St Mary, Blymhill

St Mary's church (Fig.211) stands prominently on a knoll overlooking the fairly flat countryside of the Staffordshire-Shropshire border, just 1½ miles north of Weston-under-Lizard. It was founded in the twelfth century as a chapel-of-ease to the collegiate church of Gnosall, but soon acquired independent parochial status.

(Fig 210) **St John the Baptist, Ashley** *The Victorian interior.*

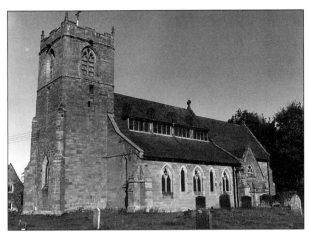

(Fig 211) **St Mary, Blymhill**

The church is a pleasing and successful amalgam of medieval and Victorian building. The medieval parts are the Early English south arcade, with octagonal piers, the Decorated chancel and the Perpendicular west tower. On the outside south wall of the chancel is a table tomb recessed under an arch. The tower, with battlements, pinnacles and gargoyles, was added in the fifteenth century. The major Victorian reconstruction was designed by G.E.Street in 1859; he made the church symmetrical by adding a north aisle with a variety of tracery in the windows. He rebuilt the wall of the south aisle and inserted new windows (compare Fig.211 with his church at Denstone – Fig.63, p36). He was also responsible for the fine oak roof, with arched braces and wind-braces, and for a range of fittings including the font, pulpit, communion rail, and the stone and iron screens on the north side of the chancel. The main rood-screen dates from 1901. The high dormer windows on the south side, which greatly increase the light inside the building, were added in 1876.

Access: From Exit 12 on the M6, proceed westwards along the A5 for 4½ miles, and just past Ivetsey Bank, turn right for Blymhill. In the village, the church is a short distance along a lane on the left.

St Mary and All Saints, Bradley

The village of Bradley (pronounced, and sometimes spelt, Bradeley) is attractive, and graced with a most interesting church, with excellent work dating from each of the styles of medieval architecture.

Externally, from the east note the contrast between the Early English window of the north chapel and the Decorated window of the chancel; and from the south the Perpendicular windows of the nave surmounted by battlements (Fig.212). The upper part of the tower is also Perpendicular, with a decorative frieze and battlements above.

The oldest, and finest, object is the Norman font, tub-shaped, and inscribed with various geometric patterns, including stars and the Greek key (Fig.88, p49). The oldest part of the fabric of the church proper is the north chapel, which dates from the second half of the thirteenth century (Early English); there is a lovely east window consisting of three lancets under a common hood-moulding. The chapel is separated

(Fig 212) **St Mary and All Saints, Bradley**

(Fig 213) **St Mary and All Saints, Bradley** *Decorated north arcade, and twentieth-century rood screen.*

from the chancel by an arcade of two bays supported by octagonal piers.

In the first half of the fourteenth century (Decorated), a fine east window with flowing tracery was inserted in the east wall of the chancel, and there are also simpler Decorated windows in the south wall of the chancel (Fig.212). Behind the altar is a most unusual stone reredos, exhibiting a pattern of cusped forms dating from the fourteenth century. A notably tall Decorated arcade (Fig.213) separates the north aisle from the nave; there are three bays, with piers of quatrefoil cross-section, roll mouldings in the angles, and a broad fillet down each side. To the south of the chancel arch may be seen the rood-loft stair.

The nave is well lit by two very tall Perpendicular transomed windows, in one of which are some fragments of medieval stained glass depicting the Last Judgement. The fine rood-screen dates from 1914, and was designed by W.D. Carøe. At the west end of the south wall is an alabaster wall-monument to Thomas Browne, a governor of Charterhouse School, and his wife (1633), consisting of two kneeling figures facing each other.

Access: From Stafford, take the A518 west towards Newport, and two miles after passing under the M6, turn left into a lane which leads after 1½ miles to Bradley. In the village, turn right and the church is on the left.

All Saints, Chebsey

Chebsey is an attractive village on the river Sow between Stafford and Eccleshall, with the church in a prominent site above the river valley. The remains of an Anglo-Saxon cross are in the churchyard; the shaft is plain below, with rather worn interlace decoration above (Fig. 12, p12).

The tower (Fig.214) is Perpendicular, with battlements and eight pinnacles and an external spiral staircase which ascends to the top. The interior of the church is peaceful and serene. The oldest part of the building is the north wall of the nave and chancel, with two Norman doorways and two Norman windows; both are small round-headed windows, deeply splayed internally, and containing good modern glass. In a niche in the north wall of the nave are some Norman stones uncovered during restoration work in 1897. The arcade separating the south aisle from the nave is Early English, with quite massive round piers, and pointed

(Fig 214) **All Saints, Chebsey**

(Fig 215) **All Saints, Chebsey** *Early English south arcade; tie-beam roof with struts.*

arches (Fig.215). The east window of the chancel contains some good stained glass – a Crucifixion scene by Kempe. At the west end of the nave, heads of a demon and a woman with headgear support the tower arch. Hanging on the north wall of the tower is a Royal Arms of the reign of Queen Anne.

A poem in Chebsey Church:

If all that thou hast to give or lend,
This ancient parish church befriend.
If poor but still in spirit willing,
Out with thy purse and give a shilling.
But if its depth should be profound,

Think of thy God and givst a pound.
Look not for record to be given,
But trust for thy receipt in heaven.

Access: From Stafford, take the A5013 westwards, towards Eccleshall, and after about 3½ miles, turn right into a lane leading to Chebsey. The church is on the left after crossing the river Sow.

St Editha, Church Eaton

The church is dedicated to St Editha of Polesworth, and there has been uncertainty about the relationship between this St Editha and the St Editha of Tamworth.

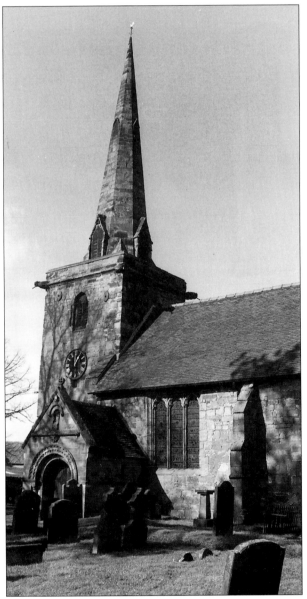

(Fig 216) **St Editha, Church Eaton**

Some authorities believe they are identical (Gould). Dedications to her include this church, Shocklach in Cheshire and Polesworth, Warwickshire. A Benedictine nunnery had been founded by King Egbert in the Forest of Arden and later moved to Polesworth, and re-dedicated to Editha in *c*.980. Early in the twelfth century, the advowson of Church Eaton was given to Polesworth Abbey, who held it until the Reformation.

As might be inferred from the name of the village, St Editha's church dominates the community, and its spire is a landmark far and wide. The tower itself is late Norman, with small Norman windows below and twin pointed windows under a single round arch at belfry level. The recessed spire (Fig.216) is later, probably fifteenth century.

On entering the rather dark interior, the visitor is immediately impressed by the great Perpendicular east window (Fig.45, p27) which comprises seven lights filling the whole width of the east wall of the chancel. Low down in the south wall of the chancel is a square window, known as a 'low-side window'; the purpose of such windows is obscure (p101).

The arcade separating the north aisle from the nave is Early English, with circular piers and capitals, the best being the third pier from the west. The tower arch is Transitional Norman, and there is a damaged Norman font in the north aisle (Fig.89, p49); this had previously lain buried in the churchyard. It is a pity that the font is hidden in a dark corner between some pews and a screen, so that its detail cannot be readily discerned. It resembles closely the fine font at Bradley (Fig.88, p49), just two miles to the east, and must have come from the same source.

Access: From Stafford, take the A518 west towards Newport; at Haughton turn left opposite the church, and this lane meanders after two miles into Church Eaton, where St Editha's is on the right.

All Saints, Forton

Forton ('settlement by a ford') church, very close to the border with Shropshire, stands on rising ground, half a mile above Aqualate Mere. The incongruous

(Fig 217) **All Saints, Forton** *Georgian nave and medieval north aisle, separated by an arcade of Tuscan columns.*

combination of a medieval west tower and a Georgian nave makes a most appealing impression on the visitor – and this is confirmed on closer inspection inside.

The exterior is full of contrasts: at the west is the tower, Early English below and Perpendicular above, replete with frieze and pinnacles. The south wall of the nave dates from 1723, and has four large arched windows, flanked by two doorways each with a small round window above. The east wall appears to be medieval, but the window is Victorian. The north wall is fourteenth century, with Decorated windows.

Inside the contrasts are no less marked, for Georgian nave and medieval north aisle are separated by an arcade of Tuscan columns on high plinths supporting rounded arches (Fig.217). On the south wall of the nave are the Hanoverian Royal Arms; the font and pulpit date also from the eighteenth century. But the chief glory of the church is the tomb-chest and alabaster effigies of Sir Thomas Skrymsher and his wife (Fig.126, p62). The manor of Forton had passed to the Skrymsher family in 1535, and Sir Thomas rebuilt Aqualate Hall. He died in 1633, and his monument is one of the handsomest in the county; on the side of the chest are represented his five sons and four daughters.

Access: From Eccleshall, take the A519 for seven miles south-westwards in the direction of Newport; in the village, turn left for the church, which is on the left.

St Mary, High Offley

Offley, meaning 'Offa's wood or meadow' is an extensive area west of Eccleshall; Bishop's Offley refers to the Bishop of Lichfield, whose seat was at Eccleshall, and High Offley is self-explanatory.

The church (Fig.218) is basically late Norman, with the south arcade showing round piers supporting semicircular arches, with plain rounded capitals (Fig.219). There is no chancel arch. The east window of the chancel is Decorated with reticulated tracery, and the chancel roof (Fig.220) is particularly fine, of low pitch with panels and good moulded beams. The west tower is squat, with a lancet window indicating a thirteenth-century date for the lower stages; the upper stages date from the seventeenth century. There is a Norman window at the west end of the south aisle (Fig.16, p14).

Access: From Eccleshall, take the A519 south-westwards and at Woodseaves turn right for High

(Fig 219) **St Mary, High Offley** *A Norman arcade, with semicircular arches supported by massive cylindrical columns.*

(Fig 220) **St Mary, High Offley** *The chancel, with a fine roof and reticulated tracery in the east window.*

Offley; the church is on the left at the crossroads in the village.

All Saints, Lapley

Now a sequestered village, Lapley was formerly a place of some moment. The Roman road from Pennocrucium to Mediolanum (Whitchurch) passed nearby, and in the eleventh century a Benedictine Priory was founded here, as a dependency of the abbey of St Remigius at Rheims. In the later Middle Ages, Lapley as an 'alien priory' was vulnerable and it was suppressed as early as 1415 by Henry V, its possessions being granted to the new college at Tong in Shropshire.

The parish church (Fig.221) alone remains from the priory buildings, and its history explains why such a small village should have such a large and impressive church. The church was originally larger still, being cruciform with a central tower. Now deprived of its transepts, the church consists only of nave, central tower and chancel. The original building was Norman, and masonry of this period can be seen in the nave, lower part of the tower and western half of the chancel. There is a round-headed Norman window in the south wall of the chancel. In the thirteenth century, the

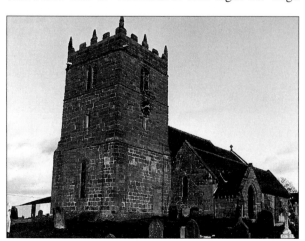
(Fig 218) **St Mary, High Offley**

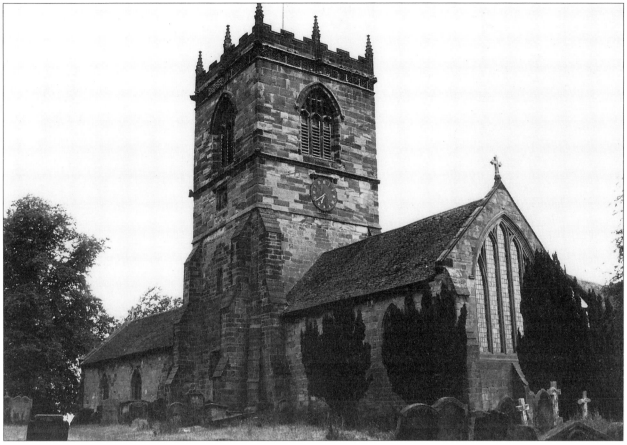

(Fig 221) **All Saints, Lapley**

chancel was lengthened: the fine east window consists of five Early English lancets under a common hood-mould, and there is a good set of sedilia and piscina of the same period in the south wall of the chancel. The upper stages of the tower are Perpendicular, with a decorated frieze and pinnacles. The octagonal font carved with nativity scenes is Dutch, but its date and history are uncertain.

Access: From Junction 12 of the M6, proceed westwards along the A5. After passing the roundabout at the intersection with the A449, take the third lane on the right, and after a short distance turn left into the old Roman road passing through Stretton. One mile later, turn right for Lapley; in the village, turn left and left again for the church.

St Peter, Norbury

St Peter's is another Staffordshire church where a Georgian brick tower incongruously adjoins a medieval nave and chancel. The tower itself, built in 1759, is rather strident but the body of the church (Fig.222) is fine and was built in the first half of the fourteenth century in the Decorated style by the Botiller family who had acquired the manor of Norbury in 1291.

There are no aisles and no chancel arch, so the interior is unobstructed apart from the too obtrusive organ. Both the nave and chancel carry a steeply pitched trussed-rafter roof, finely carved and restored to view after the removal of a plaster ceiling in 1873. The five-light east window also dates from this time, but all the other windows in the nave and chancel show Decorated tracery, more complex in the chancel than

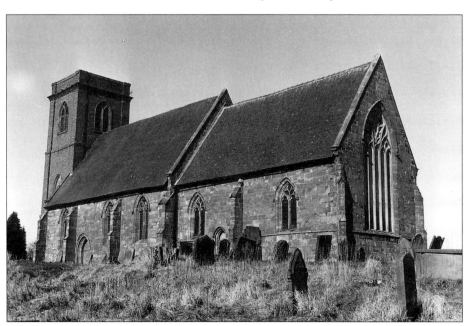

(Fig 222) **St Peter, Norbury**

(Fig 223) **St Peter, Norbury** *Tomb recess of Ralph le Botiller.*

(Fig 224) **St Chad, Seighford**

(Fig 225) **St Chad, Seighford** *The Norman interior contrasts with the seventeenth-century brick exterior.*

the nave. The font dates from 1738; it has a shallow bowl and a barred stem. The Jacobean pulpit and communion rails are attractive.

The chancel has an impressive array of monuments. Undoubtedly the finest is the brass in the floor to the north of the altar; this commemorates Lady Hawise Botiller, who died in 1359. In the north wall of the chancel is a tomb recess with shafts on each side, and a cusped arch under a crocketed gable (Fig.223); below is the painted stone effigy which probably represents her husband, Ralph le Botiller junior, depicted with legs crossed and dressed in chain armour (Fig.101, p53); the effigy has been re-painted, possibly in the seventeenth century. It is thought that it was he who built the church *c.*1340. Three mutilated effigies are also to be found: two in the chancel and the third in a corner of the nave near the font. These date from the late fourteenth or early fifteenth centuries, and represent further members of the Botiller family. The large architectural tablet in the south wall of the chancel commemorates Charles Skrymsher (died 1787); he is from the same family whose impressive tomb-chest is in nearby Forton church.

Access: From Eccleshall, proceed south along A519 towards Newport. After passing Woodseaves, the road winds and crosses the Shropshire Union Canal; take the first lane on the left after the canal to Norbury, and St Peter's will be seen on your left. The key may be obtained form the Rectory in the main road in Woodseaves.

St Chad, Seighford

In the Domesday survey (1086), the settlement was known as Cesteford, the manor being held by two Frenchmen and a thane from the bishop of Chester (Hinde); the name is said to be a Normanised form of Chesterford, Cesteford having become Seteford by the time of the Curia Regis Rolls in 1208.

As one walks along the path from the south, the external appearances of the church are deceptive: the west tower is built of brick, and dates from the seventeenth century, and the south wall is also brick

(Fig.224). But the chancel is of medieval stone, and so is the whole of the north side.

Inside it is immediately clear that the building is Norman, with impressive piers supporting semicircular arcades, and a Norman chancel arch (Fig.225). The capitals are square, with scallop carving beneath, the capital of the west respond showing water-leaf carving. In the north chapel is the alabaster tomb-chest of William Bowyer and his wife (1593); the effigies are well-preserved, and around the chest below are statuettes (Fig.116, p58). In the chancel is the Eld family pew, with a private door dated 1748, and above are the family hatchments. A panel of medieval stained glass, showing a head of a female saint, is shown in Fig.137, p64. The pulpit and communion rail are Jacobean, and the octagonal font is also from the seventeenth century.

Access: From Stafford, take the A5013 north-west towards Eccleshall; at Great Bridgeford, turn left into B5405, and after a quarter of a mile turn left again. After half-a-mile, a further left turn leads to Seighford, where the church is on the left.

St Andrew, Weston-under-Lizard

Weston Park, the seat of the Earls of Bradford, is a distinguished house dating from 1671. The church of

(Fig 226) **St Andrew, Weston-under-Lizard** *The interior, with a fine Victorian coved ceiling.*

St Andrew is immediately adjacent to the house, and occupies a delightful setting just beyond an ornamental lake. Access to the church, which has parochial status, is described below.

The present building dates from 1700, except for the east wall of the chancel and the west tower. The east wall of the chancel has a three-light Decorated window. The tower has a castellated parapet and angle pinnacles and looks late Perpendicular, but Pevsner suspects that it may be post-Reformation. The nave has round-headed windows with pilasters between. In 1876, north and south chancel aisles were added, the south aisle becoming the family chapel, and the nave received a fine coved ceiling (Fig.226).

There are some notable fittings and monuments. The octagonal oak pulpit is very fine, especially the tester or sounding-board above (Fig.150, p67). The wrought-iron communion rail is also early eighteenth century, and has been attributed to Robert Bakewell of Derby (who designed the fine wrought-iron screen in Derby Cathedral). As at Derby, the Royal Arms are incorporated in the iron-work. The attractive font is the work of G.E.Street (1869-70).

The earliest monuments are the carved wooden effigies of knights probably dating from the fourteenth century; they are on either side of the altar (Fig.98, p52). In the south chancel chapel are an excellent

(Fig 227) **St Andrew, Weston-under-Lizard** *Memorial to the Countess of Bradford (1842) by Peter Hollins.*

series of nineteenth-century Bradford monuments: the Earl of Bradford (1800) by Rossi; the Earl of Bradford (1825) by Hollins; the large composition commemorating the Countess of Bradford (1842) also by Hollins (Fig.227); and in a recess, the reclining figure of the Countess of Bradford (1897) by J.Taylor.

Access: Weston-under-Lizard is on the A5, about halfway between Junction 12 of the M6 and Telford. For access to the church, do not go into the main entrance into Weston Park, but turn south in the village into a short lane, park the car, and walk through some gates and round a lake to the church.

Reproduced by permission of Hodder and Stoughton Ltd., from "The Staffordshire Landscape", by D.M.Pallister

The Forest of Needwood

Alrewas
Barton-under-Needwood (see p27)
Blithfield
Hamstall Ridware
Hanbury
Hoar Cross (see p37)
Mavesyn Ridware
Rolleston
Tatenhill
Tutbury (see p14)
Wychnor

Needwood Forest originally comprised the area between the Rivers Trent, Dove and Blithe (Palliser) and the map shows the parish boundaries as reconstructed in the sixteenth century. It is notable that all the places recorded in Anglo-Saxon times are close to the three river valleys, the higher ground between being settled later. In 941, King Edmund made a grant of land in the area, including estates at Alrewas,

Barton-under-Needwood, Rolleston and Tatenhill. Here is a happy hunting-ground for church-lovers, for all the buildings listed above are most rewarding.

All Saints, Alrewas

Alrewas is an uncommonly attractive village, with some timber-framed and thatched cottages, an early Victorian cotton mill, and the Trent and Mersey canal threading its way through the streets. It is a very ancient Christian site, for the prebend of Alrewas was established in Lichfield Cathedral by Bishop Aethelwald in 822. The name means 'alder swamp', and it is one of the very few English village names which was spelt in Domesday Book exactly as it is today. At the time of the Domesday survey, the royal manor of Alrewas was among the most prosperous in the county.

Alrewas is dominated by the parish church of All Saints which stands in a large, well-kept churchyard (Fig.228). There are two doorways, north and west,

(Fig 228) **All Saints, Alrewas**

which survive from the Norman church, the fine west one having been reset at the base of a later Perpendicular tower. In the Early English period (thirteenth century) was built the excellent chancel, with lancet windows on each side, and in the south wall a piscina, sedilia and a priest's door. In the north wall is a low-side window – a small straight-headed window below the row of lancets. The purpose of such windows has caused much dispute: it seems likely that, at the moment of elevation of the Host during Mass, a handbell would be rung at the window so that parishioners outside the church could know and might pause during their daily work and cross themselves. The east window of the chancel was reconstructed in Victorian times.

The nave and south aisle are fourteenth century, and are separated by an arcade supported by tall octagonal piers (Fig.229); the chancel arch and tower are also of this time. In the sixteenth century, a clerestory was built along the whole length of both nave and chancel, making the building much lighter. The north aisle was added in the nineteenth century.

(Fig 229) **All Saints, Alrewas** *Tall octagonal piers of the south arcade.*

A remnant of medieval wall-painting may be seen in the north wall of the chancel. The beautiful octagonal font dates from the fifteenth century, the pulpit, communion rail and altar table are from the seventeenth century, and the fine stone reredos is Victorian.

Access: Alrewas is just off the A38, about five miles north of Lichfield. From there, turn left at the junction with A513, and in half-a-mile after crossing the canal turn right; the road winds round by the side of the canal; then take a left fork to the church, which is on the right.

St Leonard, Blithfield

The river Blithe (meaning 'gentle' or 'merry') rises near Stoke-on-Trent, and meanders in a south-westerly direction through some lovely countryside before joining the Trent near King's Bromley. Nowhere is the valley more attractive than around Blithfield, and even the construction of the reservoir in 1952 has not spoiled, in fact may even have enhanced, the scene. Blithfield church (Fig.230) enjoys a lovely situation, adjacent to the hall and set in parkland overlooking the reservoir. There is no village of Blithfield; the original settlement probably disappeared during the extension of the parkland during the sixteenth or seventeenth centuries. For Blithfield has been the seat of the Bagot family for over 600 years, and the family still retains connections with the church which houses the remains of so many of their ancestors. Over the centuries, the Bagots have been very well connected: Sir William Bagot was one of the three favourites of Richard II (Bagot, Bushy and Green), and who according to Shakespeare accompanied the king to Ireland; and

(Fig 230) **St Leonard, Blithfield**

In the chancel, and in the octagonal vestry built in 1829-30, is a remarkable series of Bagot monuments, including incised slabs on the floor of the chancel, stone tomb-chests surmounted with incised alabaster slabs (1534 and 1541), a tomb with alabaster effigies of Sir Richard Bagot and his wife (1596; Fig.118, p59), and a number of cartouches. Outside the chancel, in the south wall, is the worn effigy of a fourteenth-century priest under an arched recess.

Access: The church is not very easy to find. From Rugeley, take the Abbot's Bromley road (B5013), cross the River Trent, and after about 3½ miles take a left turn, sign-posted Newton. Just over a mile along this road, after passing Rectory Farm, a track on the right leads after half-a-mile to St Leonard's. The church is adjacent to the hall at the end of the track.

Anthony Bagot was a friend of another ill-starred nobleman, Elizabeth's Earl of Essex.

St Leonard's is basically a church of the late thirteenth and fourteenth centuries. The arcades are Early English, with round piers and plain capitals (Fig.231); the chancel is a little later, with Y-tracery in the north and south windows and intersecting tracery of the Decorated period in the east window. In the south wall of the chancel is a piscina with an ogee arch, the sedilia being plain. The windows of the aisles also show ogee arches, surmounted by straight heads; above is a more typically Perpendicular clerestory.

The west tower is Decorated below, but Perpendicular above. The chancel windows contain medieval stained glass, in grisaille with heraldic patterns.

(Fig 231) **St Leonard, Blithfield** *Early English south arcade. Intersecting tracery in the east window.*

In the nave are an extensive set of traceried bench ends with poppy-heads, some of which are original. The screen between the chancel and the nave is Perpendicular, though much restored; some of the tracery is actually cast-iron inserted into the woodwork (Jeavons). By the south door is the oldest object in the church, an unusual Norman pillar piscina (Fig.232).

(Fig 232) **St Leonard, Blithfield** *The Norman pillar piscina.*

St Michael, Hamstall Ridware

The three Ridwares – Hamstall, Mavesyn and Pipe – are a group of parishes covering the land between the lower reaches of the River Blithe and the Trent, and extending to the north of the Blithe (see map, p100). Ridware means 'dwellers by the ford', and Hamstall means 'homestead or residence' (Ekwall). Mavesyn and Pipe are family names. 'Ridware is first recorded in the eleventh century, and the prefixes Mavesyn, Middle (Pipe) and Hamstall do not appear until 1236-42, though it is clear from Domesday Book that three estates were already in existence' (Palliser). Hamstall was probably the earliest settlement, and the church is the only one of the three with Norman elements. It is suggested that Hamstall had a central position by the ford over the Blithe, and that the parish of Yoxall was later carved out of Ridware territory.

The church (Fig.233) looks attractive when approached from the south, with the ruins of Hamstall Hall in the background. The west tower dates from the fourteenth century and is surmounted by a recessed spire. As you walk along the churchyard path, note the tombs on the right dedicated to the Stronginthearm family. If your visit is in May, you may also notice a clump of the uncommon plant spring beauty near the gate of the churchyard. Also before entering the church, note the unusual Norman font on the right (Fig.234); this was poorly displayed when I visited, with a refuse bin behind it, and slabs of masonry at one side. In the font were a variety of plants, some over-

(Fig 233) **St Michael, Hamstall Ridware**

(Fig 234) **St Michael, Hamstall Ridware** *The Norman font outside the church.*

(Fig 235) **St Michael, Hamstall Ridware** *Fourteenth-century arcades and east window with intersecting tracery.*

(Fig 236) **St Michael, Hamstall Ridware** *Medieval painted panels at either side of the altar.*

hanging and obscuring the details of the Norman carving below. Surely a better site could be found for this? If the parish has no further use for it, now that it has acquired the font from Pipe Ridware, another church might be glad of it.

The beautiful Norman font from Pipe Ridware, now graces the west end of St Michael's (Fig.90, p49), and many consider it the finest Norman workmanship in Staffordshire. Hardly anything remains of the original Norman church of Hamstall Ridware, although a small Norman window can be seen in the west wall of the nave above the tower arch. The nave and chancel are a single unit (Fig.235) of the fourteenth century, without any chancel arch, and the east window of the chancel has nice intersecting Decorated tracery. The site of the original rood-loft can still be seen in the stonework, and the remains of the stone stairway into the loft are to be found in the south chapel behind the oak screen. The screens to both the north and south chapels are sixteenth-century, the north being the finer. Most remarkable are the painted panels which are now displayed on either side of the reredos behind the altar (Fig.236). These portray scenes from the life of Christ; they are a rare survival from medieval days, and have recently been restored.

In the north aisle are three windows of medieval stained glass, some of which has been restored, and there is more original glass in the south chapel. Fig.134, p64, from the south chapel, shows an exquisite fifteenth-century figure of the Madonna from a crucifixion scene, her eyes downcast, her hands raised in prayer. This is the finest piece of medieval stained glass in Staffordshire, and is thought to have come from the workshop of a glazier called Robert Power, of Burton upon Trent (Marks). In the windows of the north aisle are a series of apostles, probably from the early sixteenth century. The church possesses a rare chalice and paten (not on display) from the fourteenth century, and these have been exhibited in the Victoria and Albert Museum. Some of the choir seats are ancient, with Tudor carving. Also between the chancel and the south chapel, under a Perpendicular arch, is the monument to Richard and John Cotton, dated 1502.

Access: From Lichfield, take the A515 north towards Ashbourne; immediately after crossing the Trent at Yoxall Bridge, turn left, and again left for Hamstall Ridware. In the village, turn right at the T-junction, and the church is set back from the road on the right at the end of the village.

St Werburgh, Hanbury

This is a most delightful church (Fig.237), which must on no account be missed. In the first place it has a lovely position, high on Hanbury Hill (Hanbury means 'high fort'), overlooking the Dove valley, and the surrounding village houses are most attractive.

(Fig 237) **St Werburgh, Hanbury**

(Fig 238) **St Werburgh, Hanbury** *Early English arcades and Victorian chancel.*

Secondly, the building itself is a memorable hotch-potch of various styles in the usual English tradition. And thirdly it houses an excellent and unusual series of monuments.

But let us begin with ancient history (for which and for other information I am indebted to the invaluable church guide): St Werburgh appears to have been the daughter of King Wulfhere of Mercia, and the niece of his successor, King Aethelred. She founded various nunneries in Mercia, including Hanbury, Repton and Trentham, dying at Trentham in 699. She apparently wished to be buried in Hanbury and it is alleged that the nuns from Hanbury stole her body and that thenceforth Hanbury became a place of pilgrimage. As was the fashion of the time, miracles were said to have occurred at her shrine. After the sack of Repton by the Danes in 874, her body was removed for safe keeping to the abbey church at Chester, where it remains. That church is dedicated to St Werburgh, and at the time of the Reformation it became Chester Cathedral.

So in those far-off days, Hanbury was a place of some moment; in Anglo-Saxon times it appears to have been the centre of a wide parish, with dependent settlements at Marchington and Coton-in-the-Clay, and some believe that Tutbury itself was originally part of the parish of Hanbury. There must have been a Saxon and later a Norman building here. The earliest part of the present building is, however, the Early

English arcade (Fig.238), still with round piers and plain octagonal abaci. In the Perpendicular age, the clerestory was added and the lower part of the tower was built. The top of the tower, the chancel and the north aisle were added in the nineteenth century. Indeed the chancel is replete with rather heavy Victorian wall decoration which some may feel is not in keeping with the rest of the building. More fitting is the fine Jacobean communion rail, with twisted balusters.

But now for the treasures: (1) until recently, the oldest alabaster monument in England was thought to be in the south aisle, allegedly to Sir John de Hanbury who is supposed to have died in 1303 (Fig.100, p53). Doubt has now been cast on both the dating and the attribution (Blair): this author believes a date around 1340 to be more probable, and suggests that the effigy is that of Henry de Hanbury who died in 1346 or 1347. In 1345 Sir Henry was given a license to endow a chantry in Hanbury church, which may well have formerly housed the effigy. (2) to the north of the altar is the tomb-chest of Ralph Adderley (died 1595) and his wives. On the chest is an incised slab with figures, and around the sides of the chest are carved figures of their large family (Fig.117, p59). (3) on the other side of the chancel is the semi-recumbent figure of Sir Charles Egerton, looking most uncomfortable as he leans on his left elbow (Fig.124, p61); he was Axe-bearer in Needwood Forest and died in 1624. (4) busts of two very formidable-looking Puritan ladies, Mrs Agard and her daughter Mrs Woollocke, are also in the chancel, high above the vicar's stall (Fig.130, p62). Puritan statues are rare, and these ladies look as though they might have sailed with the Pilgrim Fathers. They died in 1628 and 1657 respectively. (5) at the east end of the north aisle is the tomb of Sir John Egerton (1662), a Royalist, at the opposite pole of the Church of England from the Puritan ladies (Fig.131, p62). It is said that he had wanted to be buried in the chancel, but his sister Mary could not abide the thought of him lying under the gaze of Mrs Agard and Mrs Woollocke so he was buried in the north aisle instead. (6) finally, the greatest treasure of all is the medieval stained glass in the east window of the south aisle, especially the fourteenth- or fifteenth-century Crucifixion (Fig.135, p64). 'In the central light is part of a panel depicting the Trinity and showing the lower part of a figure of the Almighty wearing a purple robe with an ornamented border. His left hand supports the cross on which hangs Our Lord; from his pierced hands the blood drips down upon the open robe of the Almighty, forming an ermine pattern' (Jeavons [e]).

Access: From Lichfield, take the Ashbourne road, A515, and four miles after Yoxall and shortly after crossing the B5234, a road on the right leads to Hanbury; the church is in the village on the left.

St Nicholas, Mavesyn Ridware

The church is pleasantly situated in the Trent Valley, in an attractive backwater adjacent to the old hall and rectory. Its history is intimately bound up with the great families who held the manor, successively the Malvoisins (variously spelt), the Cawardens and the Chadwicks. The earliest Malvoisin (or Mavesyn) came over with William the Conqueror, and obtained the estate some time later, it originally having been granted to Roger de Montgomery. The fortified manor house of the Mavesyns was on the site of the present hall, and the medieval gatehouse survives. The Mavesyns held the estate until 1403; the last of the Mavesyns, Sir Robert Mavesyn was killed fighting for King Henry IV at the Battle of Shrewsbury, 1403, having previously slain his neighbour Sir William Handsacre (who supported Hotspur) at a skirmish in

(Fig 239) **St Nicholas, Mavesyn Ridware** *A group of three stepped lancet windows.*

Mavesyn Ridware itself. Sir Robert left two daughters: the younger married the son of Sir William Handsacre, thus healing the family feud, while the elder married Sir John Cawarden, taking the estate into the Cawarden family. Two hundred years later, the estate again passed by marriage from the Cawarden family to John Chadwick. The convoluted genealogy of these three families is well explained to those interested in the church guide.

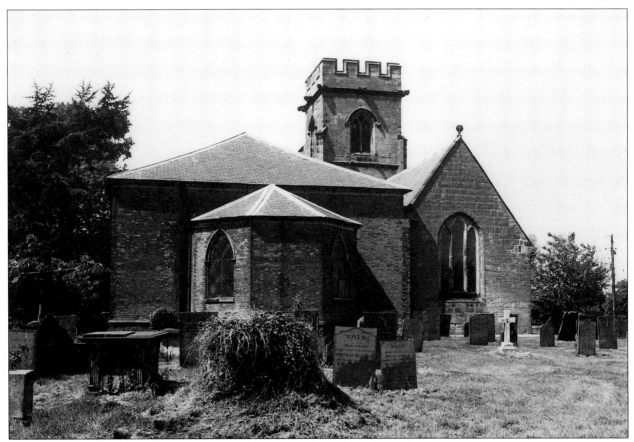

(Fig 240) **St Nicholas, Mavesyn Ridware**

(Fig 241) **St Nicholas, Mavesyn Ridware** *Georgian nave and chancel, and medieval north aisle.*

The external aspect of the church is somewhat startling, vivid brick-red nave and chancel dating from the late eighteenth century contrasting strongly with the masonry of the Early English north aisle (Fig.239) and the Perpendicular tower (Fig.240). Inside, however, there is harmony, peace and light, the interior masonry of the nave agreeing well with the medieval arcade separating the nave from the north aisle. On a sunny day, the chancel is gloriously lit; and the nave is spacious and restful, decked with the achievements of the local families (Fig.241).

The north aisle is entirely devoted to the memorials of the Malvoisin, Cawarden and Chadwick families, and contains an extraordinary array of incised alabaster slabs. In addition, there are two early effigies, said to be of Hugo Mavesyn and of Sir Henry Mavesyn; Jeavons (f) dates these to *c*.1280 and *c*.1305 respectively. In the centre is the tomb-chest of the last of the Mavesyns, Sir Robert. On another tomb-chest is the incised slab of Thomas Cawarden and his wife (1593). Other slabs are displayed vertically around the chapel; although apparently ancient, it is generally belied that they are not more than two hundred years old.

Access: From Rugeley, take the A513 eastwards through Armitage and Handsacre. Where the main road turns sharply right, go straight ahead on B5014, crossing the Trent. Then the first lane on the left leads to Mavesyn Ridware.

St Mary, Rolleston

There is a ninth-century wheel-cross head outside the tower (Fig. 7, p11), but this is irrelevant to the early history of Rolleston, as Sir Oswald Mosley brought it to Rolleston in 1897 from Tatenhill. But Rolleston is certainly an ancient foundation; a priest is mentioned as working in the parish in Domesday Book, and this may imply the presence of an Anglo-Saxon church, probably built of wood.

The oldest features of the present building are the Norman doorways in the nave and a small window in the north of the chancel. Most of the rest of the church is late Early English or early Decorated i.e. around

1300: Early English the south porch with Y-tracery in the adjacent room, Decorated the arcade and aisles (which accompany only the eastern half of the nave), and the tower with a recessed spire (Fig. 39, p23). The north chapel is Victorian.

There are some interesting monuments. Strangest is the earliest, the effigy of Bishop Sherburne of Chichester (1536) tucked into the north wall of the chancel. He is on his side, and the middle of the body is hidden by a stone; a similar effigy may be seen at Elford. High on the east wall of the chancel is the Caldwell monument, dated *c*.1600, commemorating Thomas Caldwell, his wife and children. In the south aisle is the table tomb and effigy of Sir Edward Mosley (1638; Fig.128, p62); this may possibly be the work of Jasper Hollemans in Burton. Sir Edward had acquired the Rolleston estate from the Rolleston family and the Mosleys continued in Rolleston Hall until the early part of the present century. Other Mosley memorials may be seen on the wall of the south aisle.

Access: From Burton upon Trent, take the A50 northwards for about 2½ miles, and then turn right for Rolleston. At the T-junction in the village, turn left, and the church is immediately on the left.

St Michael, Tatenhill

Tatenhill is a pleasant village on the outskirts of Burton upon Trent and was formerly the centre of an extensive parish (see map, p100). In the Middle Ages, the parish extended along the Trent Valley, with dependent settlements at Barton-under-Needwood, Wychnor and Newbold. The village now is graced by a fine early Georgian rectory and next to it the church of St Michael. The building consists simply of chancel, nave and west tower, and at first glance appears to be all Perpendicular, and late Perpendicular at that. But there is an Early English south doorway to the nave (Fig.242), and a simpler Early English priest's doorway to the chancel (Fig.243).

The windows, how-

Above: (Fig 242) **St Michael, Tatenhill** *Early English south doorway.*

Right: (Fig 243) **St Michael, Tatenhill** *Perpendicular window and Early English priest's doorway.*

(Fig 244) **St Michael, Tatenhill** *The chancel*

ever, are all Perpendicular, and are so extensive that the church is very light within. In the chancel, the windows are of four lights (Fig.243) and show typical plate tracery. The nave windows, of similar size, are plain to the point of austerity, being straight-headed so-called Tudor windows (Fig.44, p26). In the south wall of the chancel (Fig.244) is an elegant set of Early English sedilia and piscina, contemporary with the priest's doorway, and in the north wall a seventeenth-century wall-monument to the wife and daughters of Henry Griffiths. The pulpit, stalls and reredos date from a restoration in 1890 by Bodley. The font is Early English.

Access: From Burton upon Trent, take the B5017 west towards Uttoxeter. At Rough Hay, one mile after passing under the A38, turn left for Tatenhill; the church is on the left in the village.

St Leonard, Wychnor

Wychnor is one of the deserted villages of Staffordshire: little now remains apart from the church of St Leonard, standing almost alone above the Trent,

the hall, a mile to the west, and one or two farmhouses. The name means 'a settlement of the Hwiccians' (Ekwall), a British tribe. It is a very ancient site; scatters of potsherds may indicate the location here of a Romano-British farm or villa. Today, it is a very peaceful spot, ideal for a summer picnic.

St Leonard's (Fig.245) was originally a chapel-of-ease to Tatenhill and has recently been the subject of an archaeological survey, to which I am much indebted; this has greatly clarified the history of the village and the church. Around the building are the earthwork remains of the deserted settlement. Most of the interest in the church lies in the exterior, which is just as well as it is usually locked. At first sight, the church as judged by the tracery of the windows is mainly Decorated (i.e. fourteenth-century); the windows are straight-headed, the side windows of the chancel showing an unusual combination of trefoils and saltire crosses. The east window of the chancel has recently been renewed.The north doorway is also Decorated with a continuous fleuron frieze (Fig.246). Close inspection reveals however the tell-tale remains of a Norman doorway a short distance eastwards from the main door, indicating that there was indeed an earlier Norman building here. The tower is Decorated in the lower stages, but above is built of brick, either late sixteenth- or seventeenth-century.

Inside there is not a lot of note: the ugly east arch of the tower, thought by Pevsner to be late Norman, is now believed to have been constructed in the seventeenth century. The arcade is of three bays with clustered columns and dates from the fourteenth century. There is a large Perpendicular font.

Access: The only way to approach Wychnor is from the northbound carriageway of the A38. From Lichfield, proceed northwards, and one mile after the turn to Alrewas, just after crossing the Trent, the lane to Wychnor leads to the left. The second turning off this lane leads to St Leonard's church.

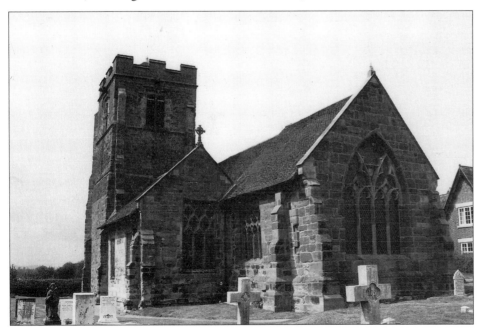
(Fig 245) **St Leonard, Wychnor**

(Fig 246) **St Leonard, Wychnor** *Decorated north doorway.*

The South-east

Armitage
Clifton Campville (see p24)
Croxall
Elford
Farewell
Hopwas
Lichfield St Chad
Longdon
Statfold
Tamworth (see p43)

Lichfield and Tamworth are the dominant centres in this part of Staffordshire, and in the far south-east corner of the county, east of the River Tame, are a handful of outstanding churches, notably Clifton Campville and Elford. This is pleasant pastoral country, as the land passes imperceptibly into Leicestershire and Warwickshire on the east.

St John the Baptist, Armitage

The church of St John the Baptist, Armitage, is unusual in these days for it is always open and positively welcomes visitors. At first glance it appears to be a Norman building, and indeed it does contain an exceptionally fine Norman font; but a second glance will suffice to realise that this is neo-Norman. It was in fact built between 1845 and 1847, replacing the original Norman church, described by Pitt in 1817 as 'a most beautiful and picturesque object, built of stone, and somewhat ruinous in its external and internal appearance.' The site is ancient, the placename meaning 'hermitage' (Ekwall), so it is likely that in Saxon times it was the retreat of a hermit.

The west tower had already been rebuilt in 1632, but the whole of the rest of the church dates from the 1840s, the architect being Henry Ward of Stafford (Fig.247). This was the decade when the early Victorians built numerous neo-Gothic churches, but neo-Norman churches are nowhere frequent. The south doorway, the chancel arch and the windows are embellished with chevron and other Norman decorative patterns; the arcades are also built in the Norman style (Fig.248). The design and building were very expertly done, and the atmosphere within is peaceful and serene.

But the real showpiece of St John's is the genuinely Norman font, dating from the early twelfth century, and made from grey sandstone. The bowl is ringed with semicircular arches, beneath which are carved

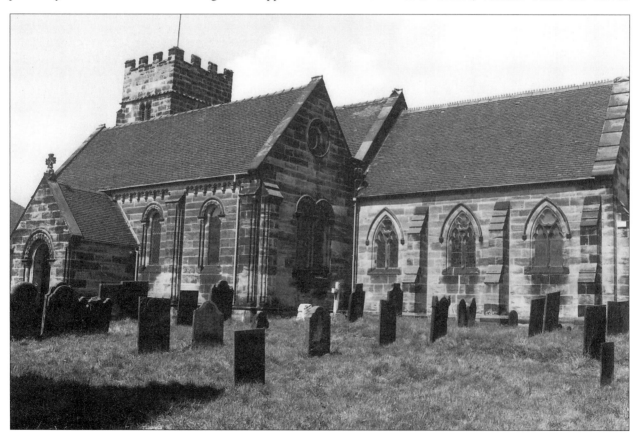

(Fig 247) **St John, Armitage**

(Fig 248) **St John, Armitage** *The neo-Norman arcade and chancel arch.*

(Fig 250) **St John the Baptist, Croxall** *The nave and chancel*

human figures exhibiting a variety of expressions (Fig.95 p50).

Access: Armitage is just south of the Trent, two miles east of Rugeley. From Rugeley, take the A513 past the power station, and on entering Armitage, turn left into a short lane which leads to the church.

St John the Baptist, Croxall

The name is Scandinavian, and was first recorded unusually early as 'Crokeshalle' (Croc's hall – Ekwall). It is remarkable that Danish placenames are restricted to this south-eastern corner of Staffordshire: Croxall and Thorpe Constantine, just south of Clifton Campville, together with some street names in Tamworth are the only examples, in marked contrast with the frequency of such names in neighbouring Leicestershire and Derbyshire. Perhaps this suggests that this south-east corner of the county represented the limit of firm Danish influence in Staffordshire. At the time of the Domesday survey, Croxall was held by Roger from Henry de Ferrers; by the reign of Henry I (1100-1135), the manor had passed to Richard de Curzon, along with Edinghall, Twyford and Kedleston in Derbyshire. Robert, son of Richard, inherited Croxall, Edinghall and Twyford, while his younger brother Thomas became possessed of Kedleston, which has remained in the family ever since.

Croxall was originally in Derbyshire, but became part of Staffordshire in a boundary adjustment in 1894-95. It is one of the lost villages of the county, and there is now only the hall, the church, and one or two other houses. The little-known church has a lovely situation next to the hall, on an ancient mound above the river Mease. The approach is through a field, and the visitor is rewarded with a simple building displaying a considerable variety of medieval styles.

The earliest part of the church is the chancel, where a priest's doorway and a blocked Norman window may be seen. The west tower has an Early English twin-lancet window below, but is Perpendicular above (Fig.249). Most of the other windows are Decorated.

The interior is serene (Fig.250). There are no aisles, and the church is remarkable for the series of incised

(Fig 251) **St John the Baptist, Croxall** *Incised alabaster slab of Anne and John Horton (1521).*

alabaster slabs (Fig.251) in memory of members of the Curzon family and of the Hortons from Catton, Derbyshire, and for its monuments. Of these, the best is probably the monument to Eusebius Horton by Chantrey, in 1823.

Access: From Tamworth, take the A513 north towards Burton upon Trent for seven miles. Just before this road bends to the left under a railway bridge, turn right and then right again, for Croxall. After ¼ mile, the hall appears on the right, and the church is behind the hall. The key may be obtained from the hall.

(Fig 249) **St John the Baptist, Croxall** *The tower: the window with Y-tracery below; the upper stage Perpendicular.*

St Peter, Elford

Elford is on the bank of the river Tame, a few miles north of Tamworth, and the church of St Peter is approached through an avenue of limes at its western extremity. In Norman times, it was one of the most prosperous communities in Staffordshire and was held by the king; at the time of the Domesday Book, there were two productive and highly-valued watermills which survived until the eighteenth century. There was a Norman church here, but no trace of it remains: the Perpendicular tower was built in 1598, and the whole of the rest of the church is Victorian, the nave and chancel dating from 1848-49, and the south aisle and south chapel from 1869-70.

Today, Elford is an attractive estate village, with some timbered cottages. But although both village and church are delightful, what really attracts visitors to St Peter's is the remarkable series of medieval monuments in the south chapel, which was founded as a chantry chapel by Sir John Stanley. The oldest monument is that of Sir John wearing armour, dated 1474 (Fig.102, p55) but now thought to date from *c*.1370; the armour and costume should be compared with those of the late fourteenth-century knight from Audley (Jeavons (f); Fig.103, p54).

Next is that of Sir Thomas Arderne and his wife, with hands interclasped; Sir Thomas fought with the Black prince and restored the original Norman church of Elford in the second half of the fourteenth century. The knight is wearing the Lancastrian SS collar associated in the closing years of the fourteenth century with followers of John of Gaunt. This has led some observers to suggest that the effigy is not that of Sir Thomas Arderne who died in 1391 but rather of Sir John Arderne who died in 1408 (Gardner). Around the tomb chest are angels and figurines known as 'weepers'.

The best-known effigy is that of the child John Stanley (Fig.105, p55), grandson of the founder of the chantry, who was killed by a tennis-ball in *c*.1460; in his left hand he holds the ball, and with his right points to his head.

The finest monument in the chapel is the last, to Sir William Smythe and his two wives (1525; Fig.107, p55); on his right, Lady Isabella Neville, niece of Warwick the Kingmaker and cousin to Richard III, and on his left Anne Staunton, through whom Sir William inherited Elford. Lady Isabella displays her higher rank by being portrayed resplendently in her coronet, while Anne has to be content with a simple pedimental headdress (Gardner). Around the tomb chest are a series of 'flattened arches with flamboyant tracery and containing small shields, which alternate with little niches containing bedesmen' (Crossley). All these effigies are of alabaster, except that of the child John Stanley, which is of gritstone.

In the north wall of the chancel is the grey stone monument to William Staunton, who acquired Elford through marrying the sister of the boy John Stanley: only the upper and lower parts of the body are carved in sunken panels, and in the middle the stone surface is left untouched (cf Rolleston, p106).

Access: From Tamworth, proceed northwards along A513 and after about 4½ miles, turn left for Elford. In the village, take the left fork, and approach the church through an avenue of trees.

St Bartholomew, Farewell

Farewell (until recently spelt 'Fairwell', which brings out the original meaning – beautiful stream) is a peaceful hamlet a few miles west of Lichfield. The earliest church here, dedicated to St Mary, was in 1140 given to a Priory of Benedictine nuns by the bishop of Lichfield and Coventry. The priory was endowed with considerable lands and lasted for nearly 400 years, being dissolved by Cardinal Wolsey in 1527. The buildings have totally disappeared, and the exact site of the priory remains uncertain.

What does survive, however, is the little church of

(Fig 252) **St Bartholomew, Farewell**

(Fig 253) **St Bartholomew, Farewell** *The plain Georgian interior.*

(Fig 255) **St Chad, Hopwas** *The interior.*

(Fig 254) **St Chad, Hopwas** *By John Douglas (1881). One of the nicest Victorian churches in the county.*

St Bartholomew, part of which is of medieval origin. The church is quite isolated, with only the seventeenth-century hall for company (rather condescendingly described by Thorold as 'long since sunk to farmhouse status'!). The nicely kept churchyard is an attractive spot, graced with a fine yew. The ancient part of the building is the chancel, dating from the early fourteenth century with an east window showing intersecting tracery (Fig.252); the Perpendicular north and south windows were inserted later. The nave and tower are Georgian, and were built of brick in the middle of the eighteenth century.

The interior (Fig.253) is bright, thanks to the absence of Victorian stained glass, and contains some attractive woodwork.

There are a set of ancient stalls in the chancel – the church guide describes these as thirteenth century, but Pevsner, more realistically, I think, says they are late

Perpendicular, pointing out that the ER carved on one of the misericords probably indicates either Edward VI or Elizabeth I, i.e. mid-sixteenth century. There is a fine communion rail with twisted balusters (either seventeenth-or eighteenth-century; Fig.152, p69) and a plain font dated 1703.

Access: The lane to Farewell leaves the A51 as it skirts the western edge of Lichfield.

St Chad, Hopwas

Hopwas is a small village on the outskirts of Tamworth, and the church is described as a 'daughter church' within the parish of Tamworth. The name of the settlement (spelt Opewas in the Domesday Book) means a 'marshy enclosure'.

St Chad's was built in 1879-81, the architect being

John Douglas of Chester. The building is situated on a slope with woods in the background (Fig.254). It is one of the most attractive Victorian churches in the county. The lower part of the walls is of brick, with timber-framing above. At the junction of the nave and chancel is a saddle-backed tower with a spirelet of oak shingles.

The interior (Fig.255) is plain and satisfying, with a facing mainly of buff-coloured brick. The roof is very fine with wide arched braces.

Access: Hopwas is situated on the A51, about five miles from Lichfield and two from Tamworth. St Chad's is a short distance along a lane on the north side of the main road.

St Chad, Lichfield

For an urban church, St Chad's has an enviable situation by the side of Stowe Pool, and the walk to St Chad's from the cathedral along the south side of the water provides attractive views of both buildings. The church (Fig.4, p9) is said to be on the original site of

(Fig 256) **St Chad, Lichfield** *The nave and chancel.*

St Chad's hermitage and his well is in a nearby garden.

Nothing remains of the original Saxon church, and the earliest fabric of the present building is thirteenth century – Early English. To this period belong the doorway, with its three orders of columns, the south arcade (Fig.256) and the chancel, where one lancet window may be seen in the south wall. To the Decorated period belong the west tower, and the impressive east window of the chancel. The north arcade and the font are Perpendicular. The roof was damaged during the Civil War, and the brick clerestory and the roofs of the nave and aisles date from this time. The north aisle was re-built in Victorian times.

Access: Walk to St Chad's from the cathedral, along the south side of the pools.

St James, Longdon

Longdon (meaning 'long hill') is situated agreeably in the Trent Valley, halfway between Rugeley and Lichfield, and on the edge of Cannock Chase. In the Middle Ages, the Bishops of Lichfield had a palace nearby at Beaudesert, one mile away to the south-west; fragments of the Great Hall may still be seen, but the distinguished house built by Sir William Paget, who acquired Beaudesert in 1546, was demolished in 1932.

St James' church (Fig.257) has evidence of every style of medieval architecture, from Norman to Perpendicular; and in addition it possesses a font of some distinction. The south doorway is Norman, and very good it is, but it suffers from being rather hidden

(Fig 257) **St James, Longdon**

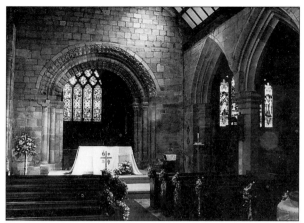

(Fig 258) **St James, Longdon** *Norman chancel arch; Decorated east window (reticulated tracery); Perpendicular south arcade.*

by the porch. Not so the Norman chancel arch (Fig.15, p14), which prominently sets the tone for the whole interior (Fig.258), and which is agreeably illuminated by a roof window which bathes the altar in front of the chancel arch with light. There are Early English lancet windows in the nave and chancel, but the east window in the chancel has reticulated tracery of the Decorated age. The tower is Decorated below and Perpendicular above. The north transept is Victorian.

The font has a Norman bowl, with unusual carving, but the greater attraction is the stiff-leaf Early English carving on the stem (Fig.91, p49).

Access: From Lichfield, take the A51 north-westwards towards Rugeley. Longdon church is on the right, nearly half-a-mile after passing through Longdon Green.

All Saints Chapel, Statfold

Statfold, like Croxall and Wychnor (q.v.), is one of several deserted settlements in south-east Staffordshire (Palliser); the reasons for their decline are not completely understood. It might be related in some cases to flooding of the Tame valley, or to a shift from arable to pasture farming. At any rate, there is now no village of Statfold, the earlier community having apparently declined after the Black Death (1348-50), and from the sixteenth century onwards All Saints became virtually a private chapel for the hall. It fell into disuse in the nineteenth century, but was restored in 1906 as a parish church, and it retained this status until 1967. It is now privately maintained.

The chapel is an enchanting little building situated in the grounds of the hall, and is not open to the public. Statfold Hall, a house of Elizabethan foundation, has been in the hands of the Wolferstan family for over 400 years. The origin of the church itself is lost in the mists of time; in early times, Statfold, like Alrewas, was one of the prebends of Lichfield cathedral. The present building certainly goes back to the twelfth century, for the west door is simple but unmistakably Norman (Fig.259). The body of the church now seems to be mainly fourteenth-century Decorated (Fig.260), although there are two tiny windows in the nave from

(Fig 259) **All Saints, Statfold** *West front, with simple Norman doorway.*

the previous century. In the chancel are two tomb recesses containing effigies of ladies holding their hearts in their hands; these date from the latter half of the fourteenth century (Fig. 104, p55). There is a plain font, again from the fourteenth century, and some medieval stained glass (the figure of a bishop) in the small south window. There is a large wall monument to Francis and Frances Wolferstan dated 1676; Frances was a noted book collector, one of the earliest ladies recorded as such (Morgan). There is also a handsome hatchment to Stanford Wolferstan who died in 1772.

(Fig 260) **All Saints, Statfold** *The interior.*

The South-west

Brewood
Enville
Kinver
Patshull
Pattingham
Shareshill (see p33)
Tettenhall (see p46)
Trysull
Walsall St Matthew (see p34)
Wolverhampton St John (see p32)
Wolverhampton St Peter (see p47)

The Black Country was removed from Staffordshire in 1974, and has since been part of the County of the West Midlands. But historically it has always been part of Staffordshire and it would be wholly artificial to exclude it from this survey of Staffordshire churches. The area contains two of the ancient royal collegiate churches of Staffordshire – St Peter, Wolverhampton and St Michael, Tettenhall. To the west of the Black Country, and still within Staffordshire, are some delightful churches in rural surroundings, of which perhaps Brewood, Enville and Kinver are the most rewarding.

St Mary and St Chad, Brewood

Brewood (meaning 'wood on the hill', bre being a British word for hill) is one of the most historic settlements in Staffordshire, dating back to Roman times when Pennocrucium was founded just north of Watling Street; the site was partly in the parish of Brewood and partly in Penkridge. It is also a very ancient Christian site, since one of the prebendal stalls instituted in Lichfield Cathedral in 822 was named after the village. The stall has been held ever since by the Dean of Lichfield, and until 1846 the parish was a 'peculiar' of the Archdeacon. A priory of Benedictine nuns ('Black Ladies') was founded here c.1140 and lasted until the Dissolution in 1538. The area was well-wooded in the Middle Ages: after the Norman Conquest, William I created the forests of Brewood,

Cannock and Kinver, but Brewood was disafforested in 1204.

The church of St Mary and St Chad (Fig.261) is a handsome building exhibiting a variety of architectural styles. The oldest part is the long Early English chancel, with six lancet windows along each side (Fig.262); the east window with three lancets is a Victorian reconstruction. The nave and aisles are a little later, the arcades separating them consisting of octagonal piers of considerable height. The windows on the north aisle are Decorated, but the south aisle was reconstructed in a very unusual fashion by Street in 1878-80. He built a narrow outer aisle with a striking series of transverse gables. The tower is Perpendicular, and bears a recessed spire 168 feet high. There is a Royal arms of the reign of William and Mary.

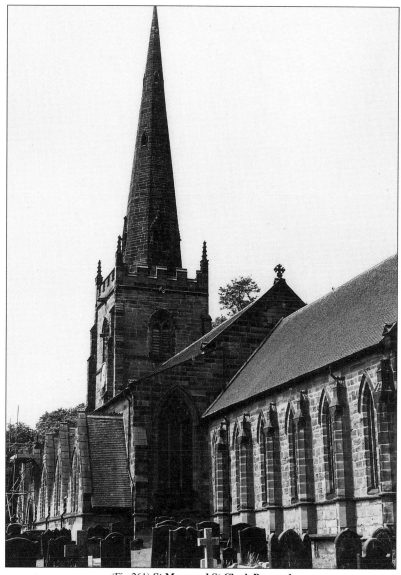

(Fig 261) **St Mary and St Chad, Brewood**

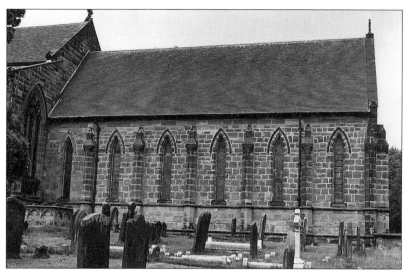

(Fig 262) **St Mary and St Chad, Brewood** *Lancet windows in the chancel.*

1587. In 1588, the year of the Armada, John Giffard was imprisoned in London, and made his submission, acknowledging Her Majesty to be his only and undoubted Sovereign Lady and Queen, but he nevertheless spent many years in prison, and died in 1613. His heir, Walter Giffard, twelfth Lord of Chillington (tomb B), was also a recusant; he died in 1632. Another Giffard, not commemorated in Brewood, was involved in the escape of Charles II after the battle of Worcester in 1651; Boscobel, a few miles away in Shropshire, belonged to this branch of the family. The head of the Giffard family remained a Roman Catholic until 1861.

There is one other monument of note in the west end of the south aisle: an alabaster wall-tablet to Edward Moreton of Engleton and his son Matthew, who died in 1630 and 1669 respectively; it consists of two tiers of kneeling couples facing each other on each side of a prayer-desk, with rows of kneeling offspring below (Fig.132, p62). This Protestant memorial makes a marked contrast with the Catholic Giffard tombs. Matthew Moreton was one of the trustees of the Grammar School which had been founded in the reign of Mary I.

Access: From Junction 12 of the M6, proceed westwards along A5 for two miles, and then turn left for Brewood. At the T-junction in the village centre, turn right, then left for the church.

But the outstanding feature of Brewood church is the series of four altar tombs commemorating members of the Giffard family in the sixteenth and seventeenth centuries. This extraordinary family can trace its ancestry back to Normandy in the tenth century; one came over with William the Conqueror, and the Giffards have held Chillington, two miles south-west from Brewood, from 1178 until the present day. The village of Chillington was removed in the eighteenth century in the extension of the park. The monuments in the chancel are: on the south side of the chancel, (tomb A) Sir John Giffard (died 1556) with two wives, and on the side figures of one son, four daughters and thirteen babies in swaddling clothes; and further from the altar (tomb B) Walter Giffard (died 1632) and his wife, the sides of the chest being carved with arcades and no figures; on the north side of the chancel, nearer to the altar, (tomb C) Sir Thomas Giffard (died 1560) with two wives, the sides of the chest showing seventeen offspring including four swaddled infants (Fig.113, p58); and further from the altar (tomb D) John Giffard (died 1613) with his wife, with their fourteen children around the sides (Fig.123, p60).

During these troublous times, these four gentlemen had chequered careers. Sir John Giffard (1466-1556), ninth Lord of Chillington (tomb A), was Henry VIII's standard-bearer in France in 1513 and was at the meeting of Henry with François I, King of France, at the Field of the Cloth of Gold in 1520. Sir Thomas Giffard (died 1560), tenth Lord of Chillington (tomb C), was High Sheriff of Staffordshire and a knight of the shire in Parliament. His son, John Giffard, eleventh Lord of Chillington (tomb D), though a Catholic, received Queen Elizabeth at Chillington in 1576; in 1585, the Earl of Essex recommended that Mary Queen of Scots, imprisoned at Tutbury, should be moved to Chillington rather than to Chartley. One of John's sons, Gilbert, played a notorious role as a double agent, being employed by Queen Elizabeth's secretary of state Sir Francis Walsingham in the interception of messages which led to the discovery of the Babington plot and to the execution of Mary in

St Mary, Enville

St Mary's, Enville, is among the first rank of Staffordshire churches because of the quality of its

(Fig 264) **St Mary, Enville** *The nave and chancel.*

artefacts, notably the misericords, the effigy of the priest and the Grey monument. But from the outside, it is the Victorian tower which impresses (Fig.263): designed by Sir George Gilbert Scott in the 1870s, it

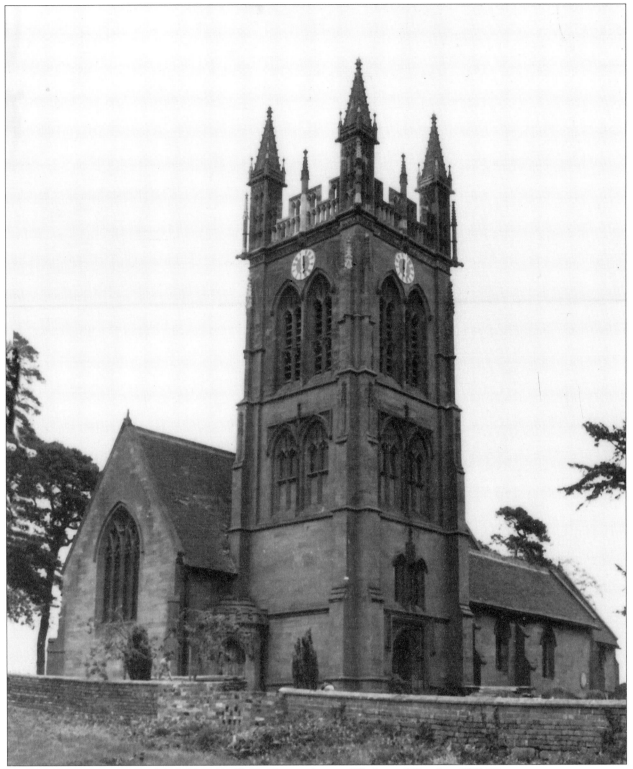

(Fig 263) **St Mary, Enville** *The 'Somerset' tower of Sir George Gilbert Scott (1872-75).*

would seem more at home in Somerset than Staffordshire – but that is a compliment, for Somerset towers are generally reckoned the finest in the country.

Internally (Fig.264), the south arcade is Norman, with massive piers and square scalloped capitals. On either side of one of the spandrels of this arcade are remarkable carvings of ecclesiastical figures which are of obscure origin, probably Norman, but they could just be earlier (Fig.265). One figure clearly represents a bishop, but the interpretation of the other is uncertain. The north arcade is later – still with rounded arches, but with no original detail surviving. In the south aisle is the monument to Thomas Grey (1559; Fig.112, p57) and his wife, Anne. This is a good alabaster product from the Royley workshop, with two recumbent effigies on the chest, and around the sides a series of upright effigies portraying the Greys' children.

In the north wall of the chancel is a well-preserved stone effigy of a priest, Roger de Bermingham, Rector from 1272-1307 (Fig.97, p52). He is said to have built the chancel and the south aisle. But the best objects in

(Fig 265a, b) **St Mary, Enville** *Norman sculptures.*

(Fig 267) **St Peter, Kinver** *The north arcade from the modern north aisle.*

St Mary's are the four misericords in the chancel stalls; these display the finest wood-carving in any Staffordshire church and depict Sir Ywain at a castle gate, two dogs attacking a bear, a couple in a pew, and a seated angel under a canopy (fig.159, p70).

Access: Enville is on the A458 between Bridgnorth and Stourbridge, about three miles west of Stourton.

St Peter, Kinver

The large village (or small town) of Kinver, in the far south-western corner of Staffordshire, is set in lovely countryside, and towering above it is Kinver Edge, the site of an Iron Age hill-fort. Throughout the Middle Ages, there was a Royal forest of Kinver, which provided the Crown with revenue from the sale of deer and timber. Much of the Edge is now owned by the National Trust, and St Peter's church (Fig.266) is sited prominently on its eastern extremity.

There was a Norman church here, but few traces remain: the Norman buttresses on each side of the tower indicate the end of the north and south walls of the Norman nave; and to the north of the chancel arch is a small staircase which previously gave access to the rood-screen. The church is built of a warm red sandstone, the tower being Decorated (fourteenth century), and the nave and chancel Perpendicular (fifteenth century). The south arcade of the nave is original, the north Victorian. The graceful font is octagonal (Fig.269), with much ornamentation of the various panels indicating a high standard of

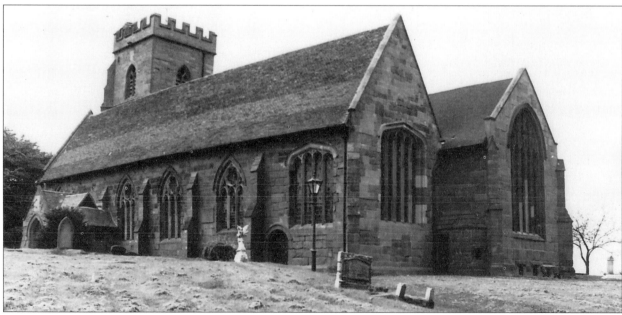

(Fig 266) **St Peter, Kinver**

(Fig 269) **St Peter, Kinver** *The fourteenth-century font.*

(Fig 268) **St Peter, Kinver** *Brass of Sir Edward Grey and his family (1528).*

unusual: it consists of a series of trussed rafters braced by collar-beams, without any longitudinal timbers.

The Perpendicular chancel is flanked by even later chapels, which probably date from the early sixteenth century. In the south chapel are a piscina and three ogee-headed sedilia; also, here is the great treasure of Kinver church, the tomb-chest of Sir Edward Grey (1528), on the surface of which are fine brasses to Sir Edward, his two wives, seven sons and ten daughters (Fig.268). In the north chancel chapel is the mutilated alabaster effigy of John Hampton, a courtier of King Henry VI.

The north aisle was originally built in 1857, but one hundred years later it was found to be unsafe, and in 1975 it was replaced by a modern structure designed by a local architect, John Greaves Smith (Fig.267). This fine addition to the church harmonises surprisingly well with the medieval building and now houses an excellent display of local history.

Access: From Wolverhampton, take the A449 south towards Kidderminster, and at Stourton turn right into the A458, signposted Bridgnorth. After 1½ miles, turn left for Kinver and proceed along High Street, then climbing steeply up Church Hill for St Peter's, which can be readily seen standing sentinel above the town.

fourteenth-century craftsmanship. Above the font a lantern containing Victorian glass has recently been hung. There is a good Jacobean pulpit bearing the date 1625. The fifteenth-century nave roof is striking and

(Fig 270) **St Mary, Patshull** *By James Gibbs (1743).*

St Mary, Patshull

'Ichabod! – the glory has departed', the visitor may well exclaim on first seeing St Mary's, Patshull. Yet such a judgement is too sweeping. It is true that obelisks to the south of the church are damaged, and the wrought-iron gates decayed, but when we visited Patshull on a sunny September day the scene was entrancing. For the church, now in the care of the Redundant Churches Fund, has an enviable setting beside an artificial lake, just south of the hall, and it is a dignified building, designed by James Gibbs, the same architect who built All Saints, Derby (now the cathedral, 1725) and St Martin-in-the-fields, 1722-26). Patshull is later, 1743, and the neighbouring hall later still, 1750.

There has been a church in Patshull since the thirteenth century, and from 1272 to 1535 it was held by Launde Priory, Leicestershire (Simkin); until the Reformation it was a dependent chapel of Pattingham, but then became independent. In 1663, the patronage passed to the Astley family, and later Patshull became the family seat of the Pigots and then of the Earls of Dartmouth.

The church is built of red sandstone in the Italian manner, with a west tower surmounted by a Victorian cupola (Fig.270). The Tuscan south porch opens into the nave. The interior is plain, with a coved ceiling. On the north side, an extension was built in 1874 mainly to house the monuments of the Astley family. The most notable is the tomb-chest with alabaster effigies to Sir John Astley and his wife (1532; Fig. 108, p56); on the sides are pairs of small figures. Above this is a large complicated wall-monument to Sir Richard Astley (1687), standing, with his two wives sitting beneath him (Fig.133, p62). In front of the Astley memorials is the baluster font of 1743.

The chancel is separated from the nave by a gilded wrought-iron screen, made in 1893. The east window is Venetian, and in the chancel are further monuments to the Pigots and the Legges (family name of the Earls of Dartmouth).

Access: This is not a very easy church to find! From Wolverhampton, proceed westwards on A454 for eight miles towards Bridgnorth. Just before the roundabout at Rudge Heath, turn right into a straight road leading north, and follow this for two miles. At the second crossroads, turn right towards Pattingham, and almost immediately left. This unmarked track passes the end of the lakes, skirting a golf course. The church is on the left after about one mile.

St Chad, Pattingham

Pattingham has now become really a commuter village for Wolverhampton, but in spite of this it is still an attractive place and is graced by its medieval parish church of St Chad. The spire, which is Victorian, is a

(Fig 271) **St Chad, Pattingham** *The spire is by Sir George Gilbert Scott.*

landmark for a large area along the Shropshire border; it has two sets of pinnacles and is supported by flying buttresses (Fig.271).

But the body of the church, of course, goes a long way back. The oldest part is the Norman north arcade, with round piers and capitals and round arches (Fig.272). The south arcade has pointed arches, and is supposed to be Early English, though much restored. The finest part of the church is the Early English chancel, which is spacious and has lancet windows, with sedilia and piscina on the south wall. The reredos, of alabaster, with a glass mosaic of Christ in Majesty, was erected by the fifth Earl of Dartmouth, of nearby

(Fig 272) **St Chad, Pattingham**
Norman north arcade, Royal arms of Queen Anne above the tower arch.

(Fig 274) **All Saints, Trysull** *The arcades and roof trusses.*

Patshull. The west tower was built into the body of the church in the fourteenth century. On the wall above the tower arch are the Royal Arms of Queen Anne. Near the octagonal font, with its unusual cover depending from a system

(Fig 273) **St Chad, Pattingham**
Octagonal seventeenth-century font.

of pulleys (Fig.273), is a stone book-rest used for public readings of the Bible; this is, to the best of my knowledge, unique in Staffordshire, though a number exist in Derbyshire. Outside, along the south wall are two scratch dials or 'Mass clocks' dating from the fourteenth century; the nearby 'Decorated' window is, in fact, Victorian.

Access: From Wolverhampton, take the A41 north-westwards to Tettenhall; just after crossing the Staffordshire and Worcestershire canal and the B4161, turn left into a road which leads to Pattingham after seven miles. In the village, go straight over the crossroads, and immediately the church will be seen a short distance along a road on the right.

All Saints, Trysull

Trysull is another village within easy reach of Wolverhampton, yet still a genuine community. The parish church of All Saints is notable mainly for some

fine woodwork. The church, of red sandstone, is mainly thirteenth and fourteenth century, with the tower somewhat later.

The interior is harmonious, in spite of the lack of congruity between the arches of the arcades and the windows. The arcades are low, and Early English, with short piers, the north round and the south octagonal (Fig.274). Above are two Perpendicular roof trusses, with four queen-posts and trefoil decoration. The east window of the south aisle has early Decorated intersecting tracery; the more complicated flowing tracery of the chancel east window is later, but still in the Decorated style. There are two small panels of fine medieval stained glass in this window. The Perpendicular font is octagonal, with quatrefoil patterning.

The screen separating nave and chancel is Perpendicular, with pierced panelling (Fig.143, p66). Later are the fine Jacobean pulpit (Fig.147, p67), carved with blank arcading surmounted by arabesque panels, and an excellent chest and chair.

Access: From Wolverhampton, take the A449 south towards Kidderminster. At the second roundabout (the junction with the A463), turn right, skirting north of Wombourne, for Trysull. The church is at the crossroads in the village.

Glossary

Abacus: a flat slab above a capital.

Achievement: a display of armorial bearings.

Advowson: the right of presentation of a priest to a church.

Ambulatory: an enclosed walkway.

Apse: the semicircular or rectangular end of the chancel.

Arcade: a range of arches supported by piers or columns.

Arch: curved supporting structure, made of wedge-shaped sections.

Aumbry: a recess or cupboard to hold the vessels for Mass or Communion.

Ball-flower: Ornamentation used in the Decorated period consisting of a globular flower of three petals enclosing a small ball.

Balustrade: a series of short columns, usually supporting a railing.

Bay: the space between the columns of an arcade.

Beak-head: a Norman ornamental motif, with stylised heads of birds or animals with long beaks pointing downwards, used on arches or above doorways.

Billet: a Norman ornamental motif with short raised rectangles placed at regular intervals.

Boss: a projection placed at the intersection of the ribs of a vault or roof.

Box-pew: a pew with a tall wooden enclosure.

Broach-spire: a spire at the base of which are sloping half-pyramids of stone to effect the transition from a square tower to an octagonal spire.

Buttress: a mass of masonry projecting from or built against a wall to give extra strength.

Cable-moulding: moulding resembling a twisted cord.

Capital: the top part of a pier or column.

Carucate: the land a team of oxen can plough in a season.

Ceilure: an embellished part of the roof above the rood screen.

Chancel: the east end of the church in which the altar is placed.

Chancel arch: an arch at the east end of the nave opening into the chancel.

Chantry chapel: a chapel endowed for the saying of Masses for the soul(s) of the founder(s) after death.

Chapel-of-ease: a chapel for worshippers at some distance from the parish church.

Chapelry: the jurisdiction of a chapel.

Chevron: Norman zigzag moulding on arches or windows.

Clerestory: an upper storey of the walls of the nave pierced by windows to give additional light.

Collar-beam: a tie-beam applied higher up the slope of a roof.

Collar-braced: collar-beams supported by curved timbers.

Colonnade: a row of columns.

Colonnette: a small column.

Corbel: a block of stone projecting from a wall, often supporting beams of the roof from its horizontal upper surface.

Corbel-table: a series of corbels.

Corinthian columns: one of the Orders of classical architecture.

Crocket: decorative projections on the sloping sides of spires, pinnacles, etc.

Crossing: in a cruciform church, the space at the intersection of the nave, chancel and transepts.

Cupola: a domed or polygonal turret crowning a roof.

Curvilinear: see Tracery.

Cushion: in Norman architecture, the rounding-off of the lower angles of the capital to the circular pier below.

Cusp: a tooth-like ornament found in Gothic tracery.

Dado: the lower part of the screen.

Decorated: historical division of English Gothic architecture, covering the first half of the fourteenth century.

Dog-tooth: late Norman and Early English decoration consisting of a series of ornamental square pyramids.

Doom: a picture of the Last Judgement.

Dormer window: an upright window projecting from a sloping roof.

Drip-stone: see Hood-mould.

Early English: historical division of English Gothic architecture, covering the thirteenth century.

Easter sepulchre: a recess in the north wall of the chancel used to house the consecrated Host between Maundy Thursday and Easter Day.

Fan-vault: see Vault.

Fee: a grant of land for feudal service.

Fillet: a narrow flat band running down a shaft.

Fret: ornamental network.

Frieze: a decorated band along the top of the tower.

Gargoyle: a stone water-spout draining a gutter, often grotesquely carved.

Geometrical: see Tracery.

Gothic: the style of architecture characterised by pointed arches, sub-divided into Early English, Decorated and Perpendicular.

Greek key: a fret pattern.

Grisaille: greyish tints in stained glass.

Half-timbered: see Timber-framing.

Hammer-beam: a horizontal beam projecting from the wall, carrying arched braces and struts.

Hatchment: the arms of a deceased person placed in a lozenge-shaped frame.

Herring-bone masonry: in which the component blocks are laid diagonally, alternate courses lying in opposing directions making a zigzag pattern on the face of a wall.

Hood-mould: projecting moulding over a door or window to throw off water.

Ionic columns: one of the Orders of classical architecture.

Jamb: the straight side of an archway, doorway or window.

Keeling: moulding whose outline in section is like the keel of a ship.

Lancet window: the tall, narrow, pointed window of the Early English period.

Lantern: an open structure surmounting the crossing, with windows all round.

Light: a vertical division of a window.

Lintel: a horizontal stone over a doorway.

Long-and-short work: corner-stones placed with their long axes alternately upright and horizontal.

Misericords: a bracket on the underside of a hinged seat in the choir-stalls, providing the occupant with some support while standing.

Mullions: vertical stone bars dividing a window into 'lights'.

Nail-head: Early English ornamentation consisting of small pyramids regularly repeated.

Narthex: a vestibule at the western end of a church.

Nook-shaft: a shaft in the angle at the side of a doorway or window.

Norman architecture: the massive Romanesque style of building prevalent from 1066 to the end of the twelfth century.

Ogee arch: an arch formed by two S-shaped curves, with the concave parts above coming to a point; typical of the fourteenth century.

Order: one of the successively recessed arches of an archway; at the sides of a doorway, all the parts of a column, with base, shaft, and capital.

Parclose screen: a screen separating a chapel from the rest of the church.

Pediment: a low-pitched gable, placed as a decorative feature above doorways, windows, etc.

Perpendicular: historical division of English Gothic architecture from *c.*1350-1550.

Pelta: a small shield.

Pier: a column of free-standing masonry supporting arches.

Pilaster: a shallow pier attached to a wall.

Piscina: a basin with drain on the south side of the altar for washing the vessels used during Mass.

Plate tracery: see Tracery.

Portico: a roof supported by columns at the entrance to a building.

Quatrefoil: an ornament divided by cusps into four lobes.

Recusant: a person, especially a Roman Catholic, who refused to attend the Church of England.

Recessed spire: a spire recessed within a parapet.

Reredos: an ornamental screen or hanging on the wall behind the altar.

Respond: a half-pier carrying one end of an arch and bonded into a wall.

Reticulated tracery: see Tracery.

Romanesque: an alternative name for Norman architecture, defined by round arches and vaults.

Rood: a Cross bearing the body of Jesus, flanked by the Virgin Mary and St John.

Rood-loft: a gallery on top of the rood-screen.

Rood-screen: a screen placed at the junction of the nave and chancel, in medieval times bearing the rood.

Sacristy: a room for housing sacred vessels, vestments, etc.

Saltire: an equal-limbed cross set diagonally.

Scallop: decoration on the under surface of a capital, in which a series of truncated cones are elaborated.

Sedilia: recessed seats for priests in the south wall of the chancel.

Spandrel: the space between the curve of an arch and the enclosing mouldings.

SS collar: a collar awarded to those in the service of John of Gaunt, Duke of Lancaster in the late fourteenth century.

Stiff-leaf: Early English type of foliage of many-lobed shapes.

String-course: a projecting line of moulding running horizontally round the walls of the church or tower.

Tester: a canopy over the pulpit.

Three-decker pulpit: a pulpit, with clerk's stall and reading desk below.

Tie-beam: a horizontal timber connecting the feet of the rafters.

Tower arch: an arch usually at the west end of the nave opening into the ground floor of the tower.

Tracery: intersecting ribwork in the upper part of a window.

  Curvilinear: tracery consisting of curved lines.

  Geometrical: consisting of circles or foiled (leaf-shaped) circles.

  Plate: an early form of tracery in which openings are cut through the stone in the head of the window, often producing a Y shape.

  Reticulated: tracery in which circles are drawn at top and bottom into ogee shapes producing a net-like pattern.

Transitional: the style of building in which Gothic pointed arches exist alongside Norman architecture; typical of 1160-1200.

Transom: a horizontal bar across the opening of a window.

Trefoil: an ornament divided by cusps into three lobes.

Tuscan columns: one of the classical Orders of architecture.

Tympanum: space between the lintel of a doorway and the arch above it; sometimes applied to the space above a rood-screen.

Vault: an arched roof or ceiling.

Fan-vault: a vault in which all the ribs springing from their origin are of the same length and curvature, and equidistant from each other.

Vine-scroll: a Saxon ornamental motif, with plants depicted in a scroll pattern.

Volute: a spiral scroll, often found on capitals.

Y tracery: see Tracery, plate.

Zigzag: Norman geometrical decoration found on arches etc.

Bibliography and References

Blair, Claude (1992) *The date of the early alabaster knight at Hanbury, Staffordshire*, J.Church Monuments Soc. 7. 3-18.

Crossley, F.H. (1921) *English Church Monuments.* London.

Cobb, G. (1980) *English Cathedrals.* London.

Cocke, T. (1993) *Ruin and restoration: Lichfield Cathedral in the seventeenth century.* Trans. Brit. Archaeol. Assoc.

Denton, J.H. (1970) *English Royal Free Chapels.* Manchester.

Ekwall, E. (1960) *The Concise Oxford Dictionary of English Place-names.* Oxford.

Foster, R. (1981) *Discovering English Churches.* London.

Fraser, A. (1969) *Mary Queen of Scots.* London.

Gardner, A. (1940) *Alabaster Tombs of the Pre-Reformation Period in England.* Cambridge.

Gelling, M. (1992) *The West Midlands in the Early Middle Ages.* Leicester

Gould. J. (1985-86) *South Staffordshire Archaeol. J.* 27. 35-38.

Greenhill, F.A. (1976) *Incised Effigial Slabs.* London.

Greenslade, M.W. and Stuart, D.G. (1984) *A History of Staffordshire.* Chichester.

Hinde, I. (1985) *The Domesday Book: England's Heritage, then and now.* London.

Jeavons, S.A. (a) 1943-44) *Armitage Font and Cross-shaft.* Trans. Birmingham Archaeol. Soc.65. 137-140.

Jeavons, S.A. (b) (1945-46) *Anglo-Saxon Cross-shafts in Staffordshire.* Ib. 66. 110-123.

Jeavons, S.A. (c) (1947-48) *Medieval Woodwork in South Staffordshire.* Ib. 67. 42-54.

Jeavons, S.A. (d) (1949-50) *The Fonts of Staffordshire.* Ib. 68. 12-24.

Jeavons, S.A. (e) (1949-50) *Medieval Painted Glass in Staffordshire Churches.* Ib. 68. 25-73.

Jeavons, S.A. (f) (1951-52) *Monumental Effigies of Staffordshire.* Ib. Part 1 69. 1-27.
　　　　(g) (1953-54) Part II. 70. 1-36.
　　　　(h) (1955-56) Part III. 71. 1-35.

Keyser, C.E. (1904) *A List of Norman Tympana and Lintels.* London.

Marks, R. (1993) *Stained Glass in England during the Middle Ages.* London.

Masefield, C. (1910) *Staffordshire (in the 'Little Guide' series).* London.

Morris, R. (1989) *Churches in the Landscape.* London.

Palliser, D.M. (1975) *The Staffordshire Landscape.* London.

Pevsner, N. (1974) *The Buildings of England: Staffordshire.* Harmondsworth.

Randall, G. (1982) *The English Parish Church.* London.

Simkin, D.J. (ed.) (1983) *A Guide to some Staffordshire Churches.*

Smith, J.H. (1874) *Brewood: A Resumé Historical and Topographical.*

Thorold, H. (1978) *A Shell Guide: Staffordshire.* London.

Vallance, A. (1936) *English Church Screens.* London.

Wilson, D.M. (1984) *Anglo-Saxon Art.* London.

Index

Abnett, William 82
Adda 9
Adderley, Ralph 59, 104
Aethelbald, King 9, 10
Aethelflaed 10, 44
Aethelred, King 9, 10, 104
Aethelwald, Bishop 9
Agard, Mrs 62, 104
Alabaster 14, 53
Alfred the Great, King 9
Alrewas 49, **100-101**, 114
Alstonefield 66, 67, 69, **71-73**
Altar-rails 69
Anglo-Saxon church 10
Anglo-Saxon crosses 10-12
Aqualate Hall 96
Arderne, Sir Thomas 111
Armitage 8, 34, 49, 50 **108-109**
Ashdown, J. 92
Ashenhurst family 77, 87
Ashley 34, 56, 59, **92**
Astbury 26
Astley family 56, 62, 120
Aston, Sir Edward 43
Athelstan, King 10, 44
Audley 53, 54, **82-83**
Audley, Sir Thomas de 82, 83
Augustine, St. 9

Babington plot 29
Bagot family 30, 59, 86, 101, 102
Bakewell 10
Bakewell, Robert 99
Ball-flower decoration 23
Barthomley 42
Barton-under-Needwood 26, **27-28,** 106
Bassett family 63, 73, 74
Beak-head decoration 13
Beaudesert 113
Beckermet St.John 11
Bench-ends 69, 70
Bermingham, Roger de 117
Bertelin, St. 10, 42, 76
Betley 29, 66, 80, **83**
Betti 9
Billet decoration 13
Black Country 8, 115
Black Death 26, 114
Blakeway, Rev. B. 75
Blithfield 55, 59, **101-102**
Blore 8, 56, 63, 64, 65, 69, 70, **73-74**
Blymhill **92-93**

Bodley, J.F. 34, 37, 38, 107
Boeck 38
Boscobel 48, 116
Botiller family 53, 97, 98
Bowyer, William 58, 98
Box-pews 69
Bradbourne 10
Bradford, Earls of 98, 99
Bradley 8, 49, 83, **93-94**
Bradley-in-the-Moors 32, **83-84**
Brailsford 12
Breedon-on-the-Hill 10
Brewood 8, 47, 55, 58, 59, 60, 62, **115-116**
Broughton **29-30**, 64, 69
Broughton family 29, 30
Brown, Ford Madox 74
Browne, Thomas 94
Bunbury 26
Burlison and Grylls 16, 38
Burne-Jones, Sir Edward 74, 87, 88
Burton upon Trent 9, 14, 55, 56, 60
Burton upon Trent, St.Chad 37, 38
Burton upon Trent, St Modwen 32
Bushbury 49

Caldwell family 106
Canute, King 10
Canwell 14
Caröe, W.D. 21, 94
Catton 109
Caverswall 29
Cawarden family 105, 106
Ceadda, St. 9
Chad, St. 9, 20
Chadwick family 105, 106
Chantrey, Sir Francis 76, 109
Charles II 48, 116
Charles Edward, Prince 78
Chartley 90, 116
Chawner, Thomas 85
Cheadle 34
Chebsey 12, **94-95**
Checkley 11, 22, 29, 49, 64, **84-85**
Cheddleton 64, **74-75**
Chellaston 53
Chester, Bishop of 13, 20
Chester Cathedral 104
Chester, Earl of 88
Chetwynd family 30, 31, 92
Chevron decoration 13
Chillington 116
Choir-stalls 69, 70

Church Eaton 27, 49, **95**

Cibber, C.G. 46

Clifton Campville 7, 8, 22, 23, **24-25,** 55, 57, 64, 65

Collegiate churches 8, 10, 39-48

Combermere Abbey 88

Communion rails 69

Congreve family 91

Coppenhall 18, **19-20,** 41

Coton-in-the-Clay 104

Cotton, Charles 72

Cromwell, Lady 62

Croxall **109-110,** 114

Croxden Abbey 14, 85

Cubley 55

Curzon family 109

Curvilinear tracery 23

Cushion decoration 13

Danegeld 9

Danelaw 9

Dartmouth, Earls of 120

Decorated architecture 22-24

Delves family 30, 82

Denstone 34, **36-37,** 93

Devereux, Sir Walter 90, 91

Dieulacres Abbey 74

Digby, George 88, 89

Diuma 9

Doddington Hall 30

Dog-tooth decoration 13, 18

Domesday survey 13

Douglas, John 113

Draycott family 56, 60, 85

Draycott-in-the-Moors 51, 52, 55, 56, 59, 60, **85-86**

Dublin, Archbishop of 41

Dunston 41

Early English architecture 18-19

Eccleshall 8, 9, 10, 13, 18, 19, **20-21,** 56, 59, 60, 92

Eccleston 37

Edgar, King 41, 44

Edgmond 49

Edinghall 109

Editha, St. of Polesworth 95

Editha, St. of Tamworth 10, 44, 95

Edmund, King 27, 100

Edward, the Black Prince 82, 111

Edward the Confessor, King 10, 76

Edward, King of Wessex 10, 44

Edward I 40, 75

Edward VI 112

Effigies, monumental 51-63

Egerton, Ralph 83

Egerton family 55, 61, 62, 88, 104

Eld family 98

Elford 8, 34, 53, 55, 106, **111**

Elizabeth I 29, 112, 116

Enville 7, 51, 52, 55, 57 64, 69, 70, **116-118**

Erdeswick family 56, 59, 88, 89

Esdaile, Mrs.K.A. 55, 76

Essex, Earl of 102, 116

Ethelred the Unready, King 10

Eyam 10

Farewell 14, 32, 69, **111-112**

Ferrers, Henry de 13, 14, 27, 109

Ferrers, Sir John 44, 46

Field of the Cloth of Gold 28, 116

FitzAnsculf, William 13

Fitzherbert family 29, 86

Foljambe, Godfrey 85

Fonts 49-50

Forton 32, 59, 62, **95-96**

François I 28, 116

Gaunt, John of 14, 111

Gerard family 59, 88, 92

Gibbons, Grinling 31, 46

Gibbs, James 32, 119

Giffard family 29, 58, 60, 86, 116

Glass, stained 60, 64

Gnosall 8, 23, **39-40,** 53

Goodwin, Francis 34

Gosforth 11

Gothic Revival, The 34

Gray, Thomas 34

Great Budworth 26

Greek key 10

Gregory, Pope 9

Grey family 57, 116, 119

Griffiths, Henry 107

Hamilton, Dukes of 88

Hamstall Ridware 8, 49, 64, **102-103**

Hanbury 8, 9, 37, 53, 55, 59, 60, 61 62, 64, **103-105**

Hanbury, Sir John de 53, 104

Handsacre, Sir William 105

Harold, King 10, 13

Harpur, Henry 55

Harracles Hall 75

Harrowby family 88, 89

Harrying of the north 13

Hastings, Battle of 10, 13

Heath 13

Henry V 96

Henry VI 119

Henry VII 28

Henry VIII 28, 116

Hereford, Viscount 91

Heywood, Sir Percival 36

High Offley 14, **96**

Hoar Cross 34, 36, **37-38**

Hollemans, Jasper 56, 73, 83, 92, 106
Hollins 99
Hopwas 34, **112-113**
Horton 26, **75**
Horton family 109

Ilam 8, 11, 29, 42, 49, 50, 59, 60, 62, 71, **75-76**
Ingestre 7, 8, 29, **30-31**
Ingram, Hugo 37
Intersecting tracery 22

Jeavons, S.A. 11, 13, 49, 50, 51, 56, 64, 83, 105, 106, 111
Johnson, Thomas 86

Keble, John 34
Kedleston 109
Kempe, C.E. 94
King's Bromley 65
Kinver 7, 8, 49, 53, **118-119**

Lancet windows 18
Lane family 48, 59
Lapley 14, **96-97**
Launde Priory 120
Leek 11, 12, 71, **76-77**
Legge family 120
Leigh 34, 55, 64, **86-87**
Leveson family 48
Lichfield 9, 108
Lichfield Cathedral 10, 49, 51, 66
Lichfield St Chad 13, **113**
Lilleshall Abbey 48, 49
Littleton family 42, 58, 61
Longdon 14, 49, **113-114**
Low-side windows 95, 101
Lowe, Mary 21

Madeley 55, 56, 64, 66, **87-88**
Maer 29
Malbanc, William de 88
Malpas 26
Marchington 32, 104
Mary I 29
Mary, Queen of Scots 14, 90, 116
Marton 80
Mavesyn family 32, 105, 106
Mavesyn Ridware 102, **105-106**
Mayfield 8, 13, 18, 66, 69, **77-78**
Mercia 9, 10, 43, 44, 104
Meverell family 76
Meynell family 37
Minster churches 10
Modwen, St. 9
Monastic foundations 14
Montgomery, Roger de 13, 105, 109
Monuments 51-63

Moorecock, William 55
Moreton, Edward 62, 116
Morris, William 74, 87, 88
Mosley family 62, 106

Nailhead decoration 13
Nantwich 26
Needwood Forest 7, 28, 37, 100-107
Neville, Lady Isabella 111
Newbold 106
Norbury 52, 53, **97-98**
Norman architecture 13, 14
Nottingham 55

Offa, King 9, 10, 43
Offley, John 87
Ogee arch 22
Okeover 60, 64, **78-79**
Okeover family 79
Orm 16, 78
Oswald, King 9
Oswy 9
Overton, Bishop 21, 59, 60

Paget, Sir William 113
Parker, Richard 55
Patshull 32, 55, 56, 62, **119-120**
Pattingham 18, **120-121**
Peada, King 9
Penda, King 9
Pendlebury 37
Penkridge 7, 8, 19, 39, **40-42**, 55, 56, 58, 61
Pennocrucium 40, 96, 115
Perpendicular architecture 26-27
Pews 69
Pigot family 120
Pipe Ridware 49, 102, 103
Plague, bubonic 26
Plate tracery 18
Plot, Robert 30
Poitiers, Battle of 82
Polesworth 95
Potteries 82-91
Power, Robert 30, 60, 73, 103
Pugin, A.W.N. 34, 87
Pulpits 66-68
Pye family 24

Quellin, Arnold 46

Redundant Churches Fund 119
Repton 9, 10, 43, 104
Reticulated tracery 23
Richard II 101
Richard III 111
Rickman, Thomas 34

Robinson, William 90
Rolleston 11, 23, 60, 62, **106,** 111
Romanesque architecture 13, 14
Rosetti, D.G. 74, 88
Rossi, J.F. 99
Royal free colleges 39-48
Royal peculiars 39, 47
Royley family 48, 55, 56, 86, 117
Rugeley 60
Rushton Spencer 29, **79-81**
Russell, Jesse Watts 75, 76
Rysbrack, J.M. 24

Sandon 56, 59, 66, 68, **88-89**
Sandwell 14
Scallop 13
Scott, Sir George Gilbert 16, 42, 43, 116, 117, 120
Screens 64-66
Seighford 55, 58, 64, **98**
Shareshill 32, **33,** 41
Shaw, Norman 71
Sherburne, Bishop 106
Shocklach 95
Shrewsbury, Battle of 105
Shrewsbury, Earl of 13
Sihtric, King 10, 41
Skrymsher family 62, 96, 98
Smythe, Sir William 111
SS collar 111
Stafford 7, 10, 13
Stafford family 13, 88
Stafford, St.Chad 13, **16-17**
Stafford, St.Mary 8, 10, 18, 39, **42-43,** 49, 50, 51
Stained glass 60, 64
Stanley family 53, 111
Statfold 53, 55, **114**
Staunton family 111
Stephen, King 40
Steetley 13
Stiff-leaf carving 18
Stoke-on-Trent 12
Stone 7, 9, 14, 32, 69, **89-90**
Stowe-by-Chartley 55, 56, **90-91**
Street, G.E. 16, 34, 36, 37, 47, 93, 99, 115
Stretton 41
Strongintheam family 102
Sueur, Hubert le 48
Sutton, Robert 29
Swynnerton 8, 29, 50-51, **91**
Swynnerton, Sir Humphrey 33

Talbot family 31, 37
Tamworth 7, 9, 10, 13, 14, 22, 39, **43-46,** 55, 108
Tatenhill 11, 26, 27, **106-107**
Taylor, J. 99
Taylor, John 28
Tettenhall 8, 34, 39, **46-47**

Tewkesbury, Battle of 30
Thorold, Rev. Henry 38, 71, 74, 83, 89, 112
Thorpe Constantine 109
Throwley Hall 76
Timber-framed churches 80, 83
Tractarians, The 34
Trentham 14, 104
Trysull 64, 66, 67, **121**
Tutbury 13, **14-16,** 53, 64, 104, 116
Twyford 109

Uttoxeter 55

Vernon family 24, 57, 82
Vine-scroll 10
Volute 13

Walker-Okeover, Sir Peter 79
Walpole, Horace 34
Walsall 7, 8, **34-36,** 69, 70
Walsingham, Sir Francis 116
Walton, Izaak 43, 72, 87
Ward, Henry 108
Warwick the Kingmaker 111
Waterfall 32, **81**
Watling Street 7, 9, 40, 115
Watts, David Pike 76
Wedgwood family 75, 92
Wednesbury 66
Wednesfield 10, 32
Welles family 37
Werburgh, St. 9, 104
Wesley, John 32
Weston 19
Weston-under-Lizard 32, 51, 52, 60, 66, 67, **98-99**
Whitchurch 96
Whittington 64, 66, 67
William I 10, 13, 44, 115
Wilton, Joseph 79
Wint, de 38
Wolferstan family 114
Wolsey, Cardinal 14, 111
Wolverhampton 7, 29, 32, 47
Wolverhampton, St.John **32-33**
Wolverhampton, St.Peter 8, 11, 26, 39, **47-48,** 55, 59, 65
Woollocke, Mrs. 62, 104
Worcester, Battle of 48
Wren, Sir Christopher 7, 30
Wroxeter 7
Wulfhere, King 9, 104
Wychnor 106, **107,** 114

Y-tracery 18, 19
Yoxall 37, 102

Zigzag 13